Perkins County Schools
PO Box 829
Grant NE 69140-0829

D1191643

How Serious a Problem Is Cyberbullying?

Patricia D. Netzley

ReferencePoint Press®

San Diego, CA

© 2014 ReferencePoint Press, Inc.
Printed in the United States

For more information, contact:
ReferencePoint Press, Inc.
PO Box 27779
San Diego, CA 92198
www.ReferencePointPress.com

LIBRARY OF CONGRESS CATALOGING-IN-PUBLICATION DATA

Netzley, Patricia D.
   How serious a problem is cyberbullying? / by Patricia D. Netzley.
      pages cm. -- (In controversy)
   Includes bibliographical references and index.
   Audience: Grades 9 to 12.
   ISBN-13: 978-1-60152-618-2 (hardback)
   ISBN-10: 1-60152-618-0 (hardback)
 1. Cyberbullying--Juvenile literature. 2. Bullying--Juvenile literature. I. Title.
   HV6773.15.C92N48   2014
   302.34'302854678--dc23
                                                                2013034896

Contents

Foreword

In 2008, as the US economy and economies worldwide were
falling into the worst recession since the Great Depression,
most Americans had difficulty comprehending the complexity,
magnitude, and scope of what was happening. As is often the case
with a complex, controversial issue such as this historic global economic recession, looking at the problem as a whole can be overwhelming and often does not lead to understanding. One way to
better comprehend such a large issue or event is to break it into
smaller parts. The intricacies of global economic recession may be
difficult to understand, but one can gain insight by instead beginning with an individual contributing factor, such as the real estate
market. When examined through a narrower lens, complex issues
become clearer and easier to evaluate.

This is the idea behind ReferencePoint Press's *In Controversy*
series. The series examines the complex, controversial issues of the
day by breaking them into smaller pieces. Rather than looking at
the stem cell research debate as a whole, a title would examine an
important aspect of the debate such as *Is Stem Cell Research Necessary?* or *Is Embryonic Stem Cell Research Ethical?* By studying the
central issues of the debate individually, researchers gain a more
solid and focused understanding of the topic as a whole.

Each book in the series provides a clear, insightful discussion
of the issues, integrating facts and a variety of contrasting opinions for a solid, balanced perspective. Personal accounts and direct
quotes from academic and professional experts, advocacy groups,
politicians, and others enhance the narrative. Sidebars add depth
to the discussion by expanding on important ideas and events.
For quick reference, a list of key facts concludes every chapter.
Source notes, an annotated organizations list, bibliography, and
index provide student researchers with additional tools for papers
and class discussion.

The *In Controversy* series also challenges students to think critically about issues, to improve their problem-solving skills, and to sharpen their ability to form educated opinions. As President Barack Obama stated in a March 2009 speech, success in the twenty-first century will not be measurable merely by students' ability to "fill in a bubble on a test but whether they possess 21st century skills like problem-solving and critical thinking and entrepreneurship and creativity." Those who possess these skills will have a strong foundation for whatever lies ahead.

No one can know for certain what sort of world awaits today's students. What we can assume, however, is that those who are inquisitive about a wide range of issues; open-minded to divergent views; aware of bias and opinion; and able to reason, reflect, and reconsider will be best prepared for the future. As the international development organization Oxfam notes, "Today's young people will grow up to be the citizens of the future: but what that future holds for them is uncertain. We can be quite confident, however, that they will be faced with decisions about a wide range of issues on which people have differing, contradictory views. If they are to develop as global citizens all young people should have the opportunity to engage with these controversial issues."

In Controversy helps today's students better prepare for tomorrow. An understanding of the complex issues that drive our world and the ability to think critically about them are essential components of contributing, competing, and succeeding in the twenty-first century.

New Ways to Bully

Bullying has existed for centuries. In fact, the use of the word *bully* can be traced back to the 1530s. But thanks to the reach of the Internet, today's bullies can target their victims anonymously and from afar. Moreover, this medium allows harassing messages or images to be shared in ways that are difficult if not impossible to undo, which means that a bully's targets can continue to be victimized for years.

Bullying via communication technologies—computers, cell phones, tablets, and similar devices—in order to deliberately harm someone else is called cyberbullying. Some definitions say that this harm must involve not only deliberate but repeated attacks. Others consider even just one hostile message or public comment to be cyberbullying if that message is intended to harass, humiliate, intimidate, manipulate, spread lies about, or otherwise hurt the victim. Experts say that the most common ways to cyberbully are by harassing, threatening, and/or cyberstalking someone, spreading false and hateful rumors about someone, impersonating someone for malicious purposes, and/or tricking someone into providing sensitive personal information in order to share it with others in embarrassing or otherwise harmful ways.

Threatening Text Messages

The Centers for Disease Control and Prevention (CDC), which uses the broadest definition of cyberbullying but calls it *electronic aggression*, reports that at least one in six US high school students is electronically bullied each year via e-mail, chat rooms, instant messaging, websites (especially blogs), and/or text messaging. According to a study by Sameer Hinduja and Justin W. Patchin of the Cyberbullying Research Center, the majority of cyberbullying takes the form of mean or hurtful comments posted online. Rumors shared online are the next most common, followed by threats through a cell phone text message.

One of the more extreme cases of cyberbullying via text message to be reported by the media is that of Justine Williams of Massachusetts. A cancer survivor, in 2011 at the age of fourteen she began receiving anonymous threatening text messages on her cell phone. By the time the attacks ended, she had received more than ninety of these messages at a rate of three to four per day. Some of them were sexually explicit, and many involved threats of physical violence. For example, in one text message the sender threatened to plant a bomb outside of Williams's house, in another, to rape her.

Suspecting the bully might be someone at her middle school, Williams was afraid to attend classes, and when her parents noticed this they insisted their daughter tell them what was wrong. Once they knew the truth they went to the police. Officials then worked to trace the cell phone number from which the messages were being sent. The sender had tried to hide this number via a website designed for this purpose, but eventually the identity of the culprit was revealed: a thirteen-year-old girl that Williams considered to be her best friend.

"In our research, about 85% of the time, the target knows who the bully is, and it's usually somebody from their social circle."[1]

—Justin W. Patchin of the Cyberbullying Research Center.

Anonymous "Friends"

It is not unusual for the bully to be someone the victim knows, particularly where teens are involved. Patchin reports, "In our research, about 85% of the time, the target knows who the bully is, and it's usually somebody from their social circle."[1] Similarly, a survey conducted by researchers at the University of California at Los Angeles (UCLA) in 2008 found that 73 percent of teens who reported being cyberbullied said they knew, or were almost positive they knew, who was bullying them. But a study conducted by cyberbullying expert Michelle Ybarra found that 69 percent of cyberbullying victims did not know their harasser, whereas 84 percent of cyberbullies did know their victim. Based on her research, Ybarra states, "Few youth who reported being a target of Internet aggression reported knowing the harasser in person."[2]

In some of these cases, victims cannot believe their attacker might be someone they know, because people posting anonymously online often behave differently than they do in face-to-face interactions. In part this is because, as John Carr of the Children's Charities' Coalition for Internet Safety in London notes, "On the playground, seeing the stress and pain of the victim face to face can act as an inhibitor to some degree. In cyberspace, where there is no visual contact, you get more extreme behaviour."[3] This is true even when the online interaction is between strangers. *New York Times* columnist Lisa Belkin reports, "The anonymity of the Internet has a way of bringing out the harsh, judgmental streak in strangers who would never belittle another . . . in person."[4]

Paige Chandler of Portsmouth, England, noted this while using the social networking site Formspring in 2009 as a fifteen-year-old. She says, "I could see people being nasty, leaving horrible comments on people's profiles about their appearance and other things. Because they were anonymous I suppose they thought they could get away with it." Formspring was designed to encourage users to ask questions of each other about such things as music preferences and schoolwork. But Chandler says she was on the site for only a short time before people began insulting her. She reports, "It was really nasty stuff about the way I looked. They were saying I was ugly and fat."[5] Yet Chandler had never posted a picture of herself on the site.

> "On the playground, seeing the stress and pain of the victim face to face can act as an inhibitor to some degree. In cyberspace, where there is no visual contact, you get more extreme behaviour."[3]
>
> —John Carr of the Children's Charities' Coalition for Internet Safety in London.

Anger and Frustration

Cyberattacks like this typically make victims extremely upset. Various studies have found that victims feel frustrated, vengeful, angry, helpless, and/or sad as a result of cyberbullying. However, studies have also shown that females are more emotionally affected by cyberbullying than males. For example, in one study of young

people victimized by cyberbullies, the Cyberbullying Research Center found that 36 percent of females felt angry, whereas only 17.9 percent of males did.

Researchers have also found that teens experience cyberbullying to a greater degree than adults. In a survey conducted by the Pew Internet & American Life Project, 20 percent of people ages twelve to seventeen said that their peers were mostly unkind on social networks, whereas only 5 percent of adults reported this. In part this might result from the larger number of teens who use social networks; the same study found that only 69 percent of adults used social networks, whereas 80 percent of teens did. More teen exposure to social networks means more chances for teens to encounter cyberbullying.

The disparity might also be related to the level of attention given to cyberbullying among teens. Patchin and Hinduja say, "We know that cyberbullying negatively affects adults too. It's

Concerns about cyberbullying focus mainly on teens not only because they are more likely to experience cyberbullying than adults but also because teens have less emotional maturity than adults. Teen victims of online bullying are more likely to see suicide as the only way out.

just that we spend the majority of our efforts studying how this problem impacts school-aged youth due to their tenuous developmental stage."[6]

The focus on young people also grows out of concerns about teenagers being more emotionally fragile than adults when it comes to bullying, as evidenced by the fact that teenage victims of cyberbullying are far more likely to commit suicide than adults. In a 2010 study of US middle schoolers, the Cyberbullying Research Center found that 20 percent of cyberbullying victims reported seriously thinking about attempting suicide, and 19 percent reported attempting suicide. In contrast, in 2012 the CDC reported that less than 5 percent of adults in the United States reported having suicidal thoughts or plans—for many different reasons, not necessarily involving bullying—while only 0.5 percent reported making a suicide attempt in the previous year. Consequently, cyberbullying expert Peter Vishton of the National Science Foundation's (NSF) Division of Behavioral and Cognitive Sciences says, "While adult cyberbullying is a problem, it's not an emergency situation."[7]

Teenage victims of cyberbullying can also start hurting themselves, such as by cutting or becoming anorexic, in response to the ongoing harassment. This was the case with Natalie Farzaneh of York, England, who was cyberbullied when she was fifteen. Schoolmates began leaving messages for her on Facebook after teasing her at school about her weight and the fact that she was half Iranian. Several of these messages suggested that she kill herself and spoke of how much everybody hated her. Soon she was diagnosed with depression and anxiety. She reports, "I lost all self esteem and became paranoid about people. I couldn't trust anyone because I found out that even some of the people who had been nice to me at a school had begun to send me abusive messages anonymously online. At one stage I even began to feel suicidal and I started to self harm."[8]

Social Bullying

Farzaneh adds that the situation was so upsetting because it seemed unrelenting. She says, "The problem with cyberbullying is that it's done in the comfort of your own home and there's nowhere to escape to."[9] Experts say that another reason teenage victims are so deeply affected by cyberbullying is that so much of their world revolves around social interactions with peers. Therefore, as with Farzaneh, when cyberbullying involves a group of schoolmates ganging up on a peer, it can be particularly devastating. Sometimes it can force a teen to change schools.

Such was the case with Brandon Turley, now an eighteen-year-old high school senior in Oregon. Six years earlier, in 2007, he was a friendless sixth grader in a new school when he spotted a message on Myspace that used a vulgar term to deem him a homosexual. Many of his classmates had posted comments agreeing with this, and when he asked them why, he was threatened with physical violence. The next time he went to school he was called names in the hallways, and this continued until he changed schools. Looking back on the experience he says, "It was just crazy, and such a shock to my self-esteem that people didn't like me without even knowing me. I didn't understand how that could be."[10]

Bullies Are Bullies

With both Turley and Farzaneh, bullying occurred both on the Internet and in the schoolyard, with the same individuals engaging in the attacks in both places. Experts say this is not surprising, because a bully generally remains a bully no matter what the environment. Therefore, as Patchin notes, "Technology isn't necessarily creating a whole new class of bullies."[11]

Whether online or offline, people bully for a variety of reasons. For example, some engage in this behavior out of a need to feel powerful, others to fit in with peers, still others because they are angrily treating others as they themselves are being treated at home. Many also lack empathy and have little tolerance for anyone who is different from them.

There are also many reasons why people become targets of bullies. For example, some are victimized for being too smart or too creative, others for having no friends, still others for having different beliefs or being of a different race or disabled. And some are victimized for no reason at all, except perhaps being in the wrong place at the wrong time. Regardless of the reasons, once cyberbullying gets started it is very difficult to stop without the help of authorities. Consequently, experts are working to minimize the chances that anyone will have to experience the emotional damage that comes from serious online attacks.

Facts

- The American Academy of Pediatrics says that cyberbullying is the most common risk for teens online.

- The antibullying group STOMP Out Bullying™ reports that 35 percent of kids have been threatened online, and nearly one in five has been threatened more than once.

- According to CyberBullyingFacts.org, in the United States from 2012 to 2013 there was a 16.7 percent increase in cyberbullying, particularly on Facebook and Twitter.

What Are the Origins of Cyberbullying?

Cyberbullying has existed since the Internet first became popular with the masses in the 1990s. However, it increased dramatically in the late 1990s and early 2000s, thanks to the development and growing use of social media, file-sharing sites, and mobile devices capable of allowing people to bully and be bullied electronically no matter where they were. During this period social scientists began to study the way that people—both adults and teens—interact online. But the focus quickly turned to teenagers because of some heavily publicized cases of cyberbullying involving young people.

The Star Wars Kid

One of these cases involved Quebec, Canada, high school student Ghyslain Raza, also known as "the Star Wars Kid." On November 3, 2002, Raza used the equipment in his school's TV studio to privately make a movie of himself wielding a golf ball retriever as though it were a light saber weapon from the *Star Wars* movies. "I was goofing around," he said in an interview ten years later. "Most 14-year-old boys would do something similar in that situation, maybe more gracefully."[12]

Afterward he left the cassette tape on which he had recorded the movie at school and forgot about it. But a few months later three

"Spotted" Facebook Pages

"Spotted" pages on Facebook are intended for people to post pictures and make comments about things they have seen in a particular location. For example, a page might be titled "Spotted: On the Train" or "Spotted: UCLA." They were originally created for university students primarily as a way for them to relieve boredom while studying in a library. Someone would spot a cute girl, for example, and either address her in a post (which might begin "To the girl in the red sweater who . . .") or take a picture of her using a cell phone or other device that would make it easy to post the photo on Facebook. Initially, "Spotted" pages comprised mostly flirtatious remarks and interesting or funny comments or photos.

But in 2013 the media began reporting that these pages were increasingly being used as a way to cyberbully. Though victims' names are not used on these pages, they can recognize themselves through photos and detailed descriptions, and many are upset to find they are being called names, ridiculed, or berated on Facebook. However, victims who leave comments on these pages complaining about the way they are being treated are typically told by other users that they lack a sense of humor.

classmates discovered it, watched it, and thought it was hilarious because Raza was overweight and moved awkwardly. They turned it into an electronic file so it could be posted online in April 2003 via a file-sharing service called Kazaa. A few days later a game developer, Bryan Dube, created a version of the video that had *Star Wars* light and sound effects and posted it to his blog. This edited version and the original version soon appeared on other websites as well, and many major media outlets reported on the video's popularity. Then in February 2005 the video-sharing site YouTube was created, and shortly thereafter the *Star Wars Kid* videos were posted there. They immediately went viral, spreading rapidly across the Internet. According to the Viral Factory, a company that helps businesses create viral videos for marketing purposes, in 2006 the video was viewed more than 900 million times and was the most downloaded video on the Internet. Many experts in viral videos say that to date, it has been viewed by more than 1 billion people.

Raza had not sought out this attention; the video had been posted online without his knowledge or permission, and he was angry and upset about the consequences. At school, students made fun of him mercilessly, even jumping up on tables to mimic his *Star Wars Kid* movements and yell insults at him, and on the Internet people made horrible comments about how he looked and acted in the video. Some anonymous online posters even suggested he kill himself. He later said, "On the Internet, there are no limits. It was poison. . . . I couldn't help but feel worthless . . . it was a very dark period for me."[13] He stopped going to school, and according to some reports, he had to spend some time in a psychiatric ward. In regard to the trauma that Raza and others like him have experienced, psychologist Robin M. Kowalski, coauthor of the book *Cyberbullying: Bullying in the Digital Age*, says, "It would be bad enough to be cyber-bullied by one kid when nobody else knew about it, but a video seen by hundreds or thousands of your peers could be devastating."[14]

> "On the Internet, there are no limits. It was poison. . . . I couldn't help but feel worthless."[13]
>
> —Ghyslain Raza, cyberbullying victim.

Fatal Cases

Today Raza is doing well; he has a law degree and is president of a conservation society. But other cyberbullying victims of the early 2000s were not so resilient, and their cases made the public realize that cyberbullying was no laughing matter. Among the most prominent such victims were fifteen-year-old Gail Jones of Tranmere, England, in 1999 and thirteen-year-old Ryan Halligan of Essex Junction, Vermont, in 2003. Jones took a drug overdose after receiving twenty abusive messages on her cell phone within the space of half an hour, and Halligan killed himself after receiving abusive instant messages for months as his classmates spread rumors online that he was gay. Halligan was also embarrassed by a classmate after the girl flirted with him online and then sent copies of their chats to friends.

Another cyberbullying-related suicide involving an online ruse drew even greater media attention. The victim was thirteen-year-old Megan Taylor Meier of Dardenne Prairie, Missouri. Her troubles began in 2006 after she had a fight with a thirteen-year-old friend, Sarah Drew, who lived nearby. As the animosity between the two girls grew, Sarah's mother, Lori Drew, asked her eighteen-year-old employee, Ashley Grills, to help her set up a Myspace account as a fictitious sixteen-year-old boy named Josh Evans. Drew initially told Grills that she wanted to use this account to trick Megan into saying foul things about Sarah that Drew could then use to get Megan in trouble with her own mother. Then she told Grills that her intent instead was to use the account to humiliate Megan.

At Drew's request, Grills friended Megan on Myspace and began corresponding with her as Josh. At first the exchanges were friendly and flirtatious, and Megan was elated by this contact. She had been under a doctor's care for depression since third grade. Among other concerns, she was extremely self-conscious about her weight. But for six weeks she was happy because she felt she was developing a good relationship with Josh, even though he was never able to meet with her in person. (He had told her he was homeschooled, lived in another city, had recently moved, and had no phone yet.)

Then abruptly the tone of Josh's messages changed. Grills later reported that, on Drew's instructions, she sent Megan a message that read, "I don't know if I want to be friends with you anymore because I've heard that you are not very nice to your friends."[15] Later she wrote, "The world would be a better place without you."[16] Once the conversation turned negative, other people posted nasty remarks on Megan's Myspace page, calling her names and telling her she was fat. Shortly thereafter, on October 16, 2006, she hung herself in her bedroom after telling Josh, "You're the kind of boy a girl would kill herself over."[17] She died the next day.

> "It would be bad enough to be cyber-bullied by one kid when nobody else knew about it, but a video seen by hundreds or thousands of your peers could be devastating."[14]
>
> —Robin M. Kowalski, coauthor of *Cyberbullying: Bullying in the Digital Age.*

Ryan Patrick Halligan

[Pictures] [Video] [Vermont's Bully Prevention law] [Cyberbullying - a contributing factor] [Suicide Should Not Be A Secret] [Suicide P
[Vermont's New Suicide Prevention Law] [School Assemblies] [Guest Book]

to e-mail a link to this page to a friend CLICK HERE

to contact us CLICK HERE   (john_kelly@halligan.net)

dedicated to the memory of our son Ryan and for all young people suffering in silence from the pain of bullying and having thoughts of
people become less ashamed to ask for help when feeling suicidal. We hope adults gain knowledge from our tragedy. As a society, we
better ways to help our young people through their most difficult growing years.

John Halligan displays a website that commemorates the life of his son Ryan, who killed himself at age thirteen after months of enduring abusive messages from classmates. Cases such as this have raised awareness of the dangers of cyberbullying.

A Cyberbullying Trial

Several weeks after Megan's death, a neighbor told Megan's parents about the fake account. The Meiers then told law enforcement what they had learned, and eventually the FBI began investigating the case. Because they asked the Meiers not to discuss the case publicly, the media did not report on it until nearly a year after the suicide. When the story broke the public outcry was immense. People were shocked that a grown woman would cyberbully a child to the point of suicide, and many called for Drew to be punished severely for the role she had played in Megan's death.

At that time, however, no state or federal cyberbullying laws existed, and the state of Missouri lacked an adequate way to charge Drew for a crime. (Even today, only six states have laws that specifically deem cyberbullying a crime; Missouri is one of these.) Therefore federal prosecutors charged Drew under the federal Computer Fraud and Abuse Act, a statute created to target computer hackers. This act is typically used to prosecute electronic theft, but the prosecutors argued that it could be applied to Drew's actions because she had violated the Myspace terms of service, which require users to register accurately on the site using true information (that is, not to create a fake account) and to refrain from harassing others and/or promoting false or misleading information.

Since Myspace was at the heart of the case and the company's headquarters are in California, Drew's trial—the first in the nation to specifically deal with cyberbullying—was held in California instead of in Missouri. About this course of action, Missouri state senator Scott Rupp later said, "Without a good, quality cyber stalking and harassment law, which we don't currently have, we have to go to federal courts in other states to make a stretching leap argument."[18] In November 2008 a jury found Drew guilty of one felony count of conspiracy (because she committed her fraud with the help of others) and three misdemeanor counts of unauthorized computer use under Myspace's terms of service. In July 2009 a judge overturned the verdict and dismissed all charges against Drew, saying that violating a website's service terms was not a criminal offense.

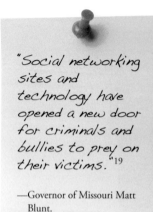

"Social networking sites and technology have opened a new door for criminals and bullies to prey on their victims."[19]

—Governor of Missouri Matt Blunt.

New Laws

By this point, however, Megan's suicide had already inspired legislative changes. Her death prompted the governor of Missouri, Matt Blunt, to create an Internet Harassment Task Force in 2007. That same year Iowa, Minnesota, New Jersey, and Oregon passed laws against cyber harassment. In May 2008 Missouri state lawmakers also passed a bill that made cyber harassment illegal. (Prior to this, Missouri's antiharassment laws required that the harassment be done verbally in person or over the phone or in writing.) Upon the law's passage, Blunt said, "Social networking sites and technology have opened a new door for criminals and bullies to prey on their victims. These protections ensure that our laws now have the protections and penalties needed to safeguard Missourians from Internet harassment."[19]

Also enacted after Megan's suicide were policies that allowed schools to deal harshly with cyberbullying. By the end of 2008, Arkansas, California, Delaware, Idaho, Iowa, Michigan, Minnesota, Nebraska, New Jersey, Oklahoma, Oregon, South Carolina, and Washington had passed laws giving schools the power to severely discipline students who engaged in cyberbullying. Many other states were considering similar laws. Today forty-four states have antibullying laws that include school sanctions.

One of them is California. As of January 1, 2009, schools in that state have the power to suspend or expel any student who engages in cyberbullying. Ashley Surdin of the *Washington Post* notes that implementing such legislation is not easy. She says, "Though many schools throughout the nation have developed their own policies, some remain unsure how to handle cyberbullying. It can be time-consuming and difficult to investigate, given the veil of anonymity the Web offers. Educators may not understand the technology that students are using."[20]

> "The problem with these laws is that schools are now trying to control what students say outside of school. And that's wrong."[21]
>
> —Aden Fine of the American Civil Liberties Union.

In addition, Surdin reports that such laws have their critics. She quotes Aden Fine, a senior staff lawyer with the American Civil Liberties Union, as saying, "The problem with these laws is that schools are now trying to control what students say outside of school. And that's wrong. What students say outside of school—that's for parents to deal with or other government bodies to deal with. We have to keep in mind this is free speech we're talking about."[21] However, Surdin also quotes experts who argue that school officials need to pay attention to threats made outside of school because these can affect what goes on in school.

Resources for Educators

While some people called for new laws and policies against cyberbullying and/or electronic harassment, others focused on creating resources for educators who wanted to prevent cyberbullying in their schools. Among the first such resources was *Adina's Deck*, a

Victims Taking Action

As cyberbullying has grown, parents of victims as well as adult victims have increasingly been taking action to stop online harassment. One of those who is battling Internet attacks is Kaitlin Jackson of Wales. Since 2010 Jackson has spent more than six thousand hours tracking down the identities of cyberbullies and reporting them to various law enforcement officials and sites like Facebook. As a result of her efforts, more than five hundred social media accounts belonging to cyberbullies have been shut down. Jackson first became interested in this cause after she joined a Facebook support group for people who had suffered a miscarriage. Shortly after she joined, this group, Angel Mums, experienced a rash of attacks by trolls (people who post incendiary comments and images simply to upset others). These posts included hateful "jokes" and photos of aborted babies. Confronted with such vile behavior, Jackson decided to check her children's Facebook and Twitter accounts to see whether they were encountering anything similar. When she learned that they were being cyberbullied, her mission to stop cyberbullies was born.

short film produced in 2007 by Debbie Heimowitz. Heimowitz got the idea for the film while doing a research project on cyberbullying at Northern California middle schools as part of earning her master's degree in education from Stanford University in California. *Adina's Deck* features an eighth-grade girl, Adina, knowledgeable enough about the Internet to help another girl identify the person who has been anonymously sending her threatening e-mails, text messages, and voice mails. This story provides ways for teachers and parents to discuss cyberbullying and related issues with children who have viewed the film.

Another effort to help educators deal with cyberbullying was the 2008 book *Bullying Beyond the Schoolyard*. Written by Sameer Hinduja and Justin W. Patchin, this book offers strategies for identifying and responding to cyberbullies and preventing cyberbullying in schools. It also provides resources intended to help students find ways to deal with cyberbullies and shares first-person stories of young people who have endured cyberbullying.

Public Awareness

While some people were focused on providing information for educators, others were producing movies intended to call the public's attention to the issue of cyberbullying. Among the most widely viewed of such efforts was the TV movie *Cyberbully*, which was seen by 3.4 million people on its first airing in July 2011. A joint project of the ABC Family channel and *Seventeen* magazine, the movie depicts a teenage girl, Taylor, who tries to commit suicide after being cyberbullied on a social media site.

Another widely viewed movie was the documentary *Bully* (originally titled *The Bully Project*), released in theaters in 2011 and rereleased in 2012. *Bully* follows the lives of five victims of bullying beginning on the first day of a new school year. When this documentary was first released in theaters it was rated R for language, which meant that no one under seventeen could see it without being accompanied by an adult, but a petition drive eventually led to the release of a PG-13 version that anyone over the age of thirteen could see.

Media Hype?

Amid the growing publicity related to cyberbullying, however, some people questioned whether cyberbullying was really as big a problem as the media was making it out to be. One of these critics is psychologist Dan Olweus of the University of Bergen in Norway. Over the past decade Olweus has conducted several large-scale studies of cyberbullying, some lasting four to six years. He reported the results of some of this research in 2012 in the *European Journal of Developmental Psychology*, stating, "It turns out that cyberbullying, when studied in proper context, is a low-prevalence phenomenon, which has not increased over time and has not created many 'new' victims and bullies."[22] He says this despite other studies indicating that in the United States the number of teens reporting cyberbullying prior to 2000 was one in seventeen, as opposed to nearly half of all teens in 2008.

Olweus's own studies indicate that in the United States about 5 percent of students report being cyberbullied, and in Norway about 1 percent report being cyberbullied. In contrast, in the United States 18 percent report being bullied verbally, and in Norway 11 percent report this. Consequently, Olweus says, "There is very little scientific support to show that cyberbullying has increased over the past five to six years, and this form of bullying is actually a less frequent phenomenon."[23] He adds that 80 to 90 percent of cyberbullying victims are also bullied verbally and/or physically in person, which means that cyberbullying is often an extension of traditional bullying.

A Michigan high school student prepares to deliver boxes of signed petitions urging the Motion Picture Association of America to lower the R rating to PG-13 for the documentary Bully. *The film follows the lives of five bullying victims from the start of a new school year.*

Lack of Reporting

Other cyberbullying experts, however, argue that cyberbullying has been underreported over the years. A 2008 UCLA survey of teens indicated that while almost three out of four teenagers said they had been bullied online at least once over a twelve-month period, only one in ten of these victims of cyberbullying reported it to parents or other adults. Researchers involved in this study also found that teenagers did not often talk to each other about their cyberbullying problems. Consequently, the lead author of the study, Jaana Juvonen, says, "Kids don't know how common cyber-bullying is, even among their best friends. Cyber-bullying is not a plight of a few problematic children but a shared experience."[24]

Based on her work, which studied the cyberbullying experiences of young people ages twelve to seventeen, Juvonen believes that millions of students have experienced cyberbullying. "Bullying is a problem that large numbers of kids confront on a daily basis at school; it's not just an issue for the few unfortunate ones," she says. Moreover, she reports, "Bullying on the Internet looks similar to what kids do face-to-face in school. The Internet is not functioning as a separate environment but is connected with the social lives of kids in school. Our findings suggest that especially among heavy users of the Internet, cyber-bullying is a common experience, and the forms of online and in-school bullying are more alike than different."[25]

As to why students do not report these problems, more than half of the participants in the UCLA study said that it was because they felt they needed to learn to deal with their problems by themselves. Slightly more than 30 percent said they were afraid that if they spoke out about what was happening, their parents would limit their access to the Internet. Among participants ages twelve to fourteen, a third were simply afraid that if they told their parents or a teacher that they were having troubles online, it would make their parents mad at or upset with them.

Adults also neglect to report instances where they are cyberbullied, unless perhaps the bullying takes place at work and their job is impacted by the harassment. No studies have been done to determine just how many adults have had to deal with this problem. However, experts say that anecdotal evidence suggests that cyberbullying between adults, particularly among women using social media sites, is growing. If this is the case, then it compounds the problem of trying to determine just how prevalent cyberbullying is.

Facts

- According to John C. LeBlanc, a professor at Dalhousie University in Halifax, Nova Scotia, who studied media reports of suicides related to online activities, between 2003 and 2012 there were forty-one suicides in the United States, the United Kingdom, Canada, and Australia that clearly involved cyberbullying.

- Surveys conducted in 2007 indicate that one-third of workers, or roughly 54 million Americans, were experiencing workplace bullying.

- The Office of Juvenile Justice and Delinquency Prevention reported in 2001 that 60 percent of males who were bullies in grades six through nine were convicted of at least one crime as adults, compared with 23 percent who did not bully.

- In the 1990s twelve of fifteen school shooting cases were perpetrated by students who had a history of being bullied.

- According to Mental Health America, a nonprofit organization supporting mental health, gay teens are three times more likely to be bullied than heterosexual teens but are about 80 percent less likely than heterosexuals to say they had bullied someone else.

Why and How Do People Bully Others Online?

Justin W. Patchin and Sameer Hinduja have spent more than ten years studying the ways people intentionally and repeatedly inflict harm on others using computers, cell phones, and other electronic devices. As with most cyberbullying researchers, the majority of their work involves the victims of online attacks. However, when surveying young people about their Internet activities, sometimes they encounter individuals willing to admit that they are cyberbullies.

After conducting a survey in 2010 of young people ages eleven to eighteen, for example, Patchin and Hinduja found that about 20 percent of those surveyed reported having cyberbullied others. In addition, 10 percent of respondents said that they had been both a perpetrator and a victim of cyberbullying. In another study in 2011 Patchin and Hinduja examined thirty-five published papers reflecting other researchers' investigations into cyberbullying and determined that on average, 17 percent of students had admitted to cyberbullying others, compared to an average of 24 percent being victims of cyberbullying.

The Disinhibition Effect

For obvious reasons, many cyberbullies are reluctant to openly admit that they have deliberately been cruel to others online. Consequently, searching the Internet for information on cyberbullying provides many stories told by the victims and their families but almost nothing from the bullies' point of view. However, a few studies have sought to gain insights into this point of view in order to determine what might drive someone to cyberbully.

Among the first of these studies was that of Kimberly L. Mason of the Department of Counseling, Administration, Supervision, and Adult Learning at Cleveland State University. Mason published her findings in the April 2008 issue of the journal *Psychology in the Schools*. Based on a review of writings on cyberbullying, Mason's work provides a psychological explanation of cyberbullying behaviors among teens. It also discusses the psychological impact of cyberbullying on the victims. She reports that two features of Internet communication—anonymity, which protects users from suffering any consequences from their online actions, and distance, whereby correspondents are far apart physically and often emotionally as well—could cause disinhibition. She describes disinhibition as a psychological condition whereby individuals experience such a loss of inhibition that they are emboldened to behave in ways they never would otherwise and are incapable of feeling the impact of their actions. This, she says, explains much of the hurtful behavior involved in cyberbullying.

Subsequent studies also found disinhibition to be a factor in cyberbullying, and some experts have argued that it is the main reason that people engage in electronic harassment. That is, while people cyberbully for other reasons—including revenge, intolerance of race or sexual identity, jealousy and/or hatred, sadism (taking pleasure in inflicting pain or humiliation on others), and fun or sport—the disinhibition effect is the primary motive for cyberbullying.

Examining Motivations

Not all researchers agree with this view. A study by a team of researchers at Georgia State University calls into question the idea that disinhibition is a primary motivator. Led by psychologist and school safety expert Kris Varjas of Georgia State University, this study was considered groundbreaking when it was reported in 2010 because, as the Georgia researchers themselves reported,

"Despite preliminary efforts to investigate motivations for cyber-bullying, there is a dearth of information on this topic, particularly among high school populations."[26]

The study involved lengthy one-on-one interviews of an ethnically diverse group of students ages fifteen to nineteen, all attending the same suburban high school in the southeastern United States. They were cyberbullies, cybervictims, and those who had witnessed cyberbullying but had been neither a bully nor a victim. Both genders and both sexual orientations (heterosexuals and homosexuals) were represented, although there were significantly more males than females and more heterosexuals than homosexuals. All of the students had a computer with Internet access at home, 90 percent had a profile on a social networking site, and 90 percent had a cell phone.

In talking with the students, Varjas and her team found that

The popularity of cell phones and texting, especially among young people, has added to the many ways cyberbullies can torment their victims. Some researchers are trying to gain a clearer understanding of what drives online bullying.

anonymity and disinhibition were two of many motivations but not the most prevalent. They also found that the reasons cited for cyberbullying were far more often internal motivations than external ones. Internal motivations are reasons related to the cyberbully's emotional state, whereas external motivations are reasons related to something specific about the victim or about the situation. For example, an external motivation might be the victim's appearance or sexual orientation or the fact that the cyberbully is unable to confront the victim face-to-face. An internal motivation might be a desire for revenge.

Internal Motivations

Revenge and the *anonymity/disinhibition effect* were two of ten categories of internal motivation for cyberbullying identified by Varjas's team. Categories were determined via student statements. For example, one student was clearly speaking of anonymity and disinhibition when he told the researchers, "If this person [the victim] probably doesn't even know me then they are not going to know who is saying those things about them, so they are probably going to have less inhibiting [them] more and doing more."[27] (In other words, this student believes that both the victim and the cyberbully behave differently toward one another if they do not know each other.)

"People have been doing it to me for so long, I deserved to be able to do it to someone."[28]

— A cyberbullying victim who became a bully.

Other internal motivation categories were *boredom, make themselves feel better, jealousy, seeking approval, protection* (a desire to strike first and/or appear strong), *instigation* (a desire to provoke, or instigate, a certain response in the victim), *redirect feelings,* and *trying out a new persona.* The category of *redirect feelings* relates to how the bully had been treated in the past. As an example, one student said of his reason for cyberbullying, "You know, people have been doing it to me for so long, I deserved to be able to do it to someone."[28] The category of *trying out a new persona* refers to cyberbullies who want to use the Internet as a way to pretend to be a different kind of person. As an example, another student told the researchers, "I was just trying to seem bad and would never consider doing something like that to

Trolls Who Cyberbully

In Internet terms, a troll is someone who posts something inflammatory in a public forum just to get users of that forum agitated. For example, a troll might post horrible things about a particular actor on a site specifically for fans of that actor, knowing it will upset everyone. This kind of trolling does not involve attacks on any specific users of a site; it is merely designed to cause heated debate and drama because, typically, the troll is bored. But sometimes a troll will come across someone who gets particularly worked up over an attack—often the creator of a blog or social media page—and decide to target that person over and over again. This is what happened to fourteen-year-old Hannah Smith of Leicester, England, who was cyberbullied by trolls who kept posting hateful comments on her page on the social networking site Ask.fm. Upset over these messages, many of which suggested she kill herself, Smith committed suicide. Ask.fm representatives suggested that Smith might have posted at least some of the messages herself, based on their research into where the posts were coming from, but police later identified one of the trolls as a boy living in Belgium.

anyone, but it's like I was really pissed off and I was like you ever say anything like that about me again I will kill you. It's so funny to think about it now."[29]

Cool Kids

Interestingly, Varjas and her team did not identify a desire to gain power as a factor in cyberbullying, although in face-to-face bullying it is often a factor. However, they point out that they only looked at students from one high school in one part of the United States. Therefore, they have called for more studies into cyberbullies' motivations, arguing that more stories need to be collected from cyberbullies in order to confirm their findings and gain even more insights into motivation. They say, "As the database about the motivations for cyberbullying continues to grow there will be a stronger basis for developing ideas for research about treatment and prevention of this behavior."[30]

Some researchers have answered this call. Among them is Jaana Juvonen, whose January 2013 study looked at bullying of all kinds among students from ninety-nine classes in eleven Los Angeles, California, middle schools. Students were surveyed at three different points in the school year: spring of seventh grade, fall of eighth grade, and spring of eighth grade. As with Varjas's study, the group studied was ethnically diverse.

"The ones who are cool bully more, and the ones who bully more are seen as cool."[31]

— UCLA professor of psychology Jaana Juvonen on students involved in a cyberbullying research project.

Each survey asked the students to identity who among their peers were "cool," who picked fights, and who were prone to spread hateful rumors about others. According to Juvonen, the responses revealed that among these students, "The ones who are cool bully more, and the ones who bully more are seen as cool."[31] And this was true regardless of the form of bullying and regardless of whether the bullies or those admiring them were boys or girls. Therefore, Juvonen says, aggression adds to social status, which suggests it will be hard to combat bullying simply by telling kids not to bully.

Hate Sites

Compounding the problem are websites that encourage users to say nasty things to and about one another. Such sites provide an environment that some experts consider an external motivation for bullying, because if these sites did not exist then their users might not bully elsewhere. One of the most prominent examples of a site that promoted cyberbullying is JuicyCampus, created in August 2007 but shut down in February 2009 after advertisers abandoned the site because of its controversial nature. JuicyCampus allowed anyone with Internet access to visit a page devoted to one of the hundreds of US universities listed on the site and post anonymous comments about the school and its students. The site encouraged hateful messages by allowing users to create discussion forums devoted to abusing particular people, and no matter how hateful the comments became the site refused to censor or remove them.

In writing about the popularity of JuicyCampus at Princeton University in 2008, Dhwani Shah reported, "The three most-viewed posts on Princeton's page—'Most overrated Princeton student,' 'Sluttiest Girl' and 'bicker surprises'—together have been viewed more than 10,000 times. These posts are typical of Juicy-Campus—personal, mean-spirited and gossipy. The site's official blog states, 'If you think Mary is a bitch, you are entitled to express that.'"[32] ("Bicker surprises" refers to comments posted about students attempting to join a club; at Princeton "to bicker" means to be chosen by club members after passing a series of interviews and challenges.)

Several students at Princeton complained about this approach to social media. Sophomore class president Connor Diemand-

The JuicyCampus website, which was shut down in 2009, encouraged anonymous and abusive comments about universities and individual students. Among students who publicly opposed the site were Andy Canales, 2008 student body president at Pepperdine University in California.

Yauman said, "In my opinion, JuicyCampus is trash. Its primary function is to create a safe haven for everyone who wants to belittle, embarrass and degrade other students by protecting them with a blanket of anonymity."[33] Student Sarah Ferguson, who was called derogatory names on the site, said, "What was said about me was just so absurd and so wrong. I don't particularly want the entire Princeton population thinking I'm the type of person who is that sexually promiscuous. . . . It is unfortunate that I've become sort of a caricature of myself, but I think the people who are close to me know that that's not who I am."[34]

At Princeton and other schools with JuicyCampus pages, some students vowed to stay away from the site. Others found that they could not stop checking the site to see whether anyone had written anything bad about them. Meanwhile, both students and teachers worried that someone who was cyberbullied on the site might become upset enough to become violent, perhaps to the point of shooting random students at a school associated with the site. In fact, a senior at Loyola Marymount University in Los Angeles, California, who had been abused on JuicyCampus was arrested in 2008 for threatening to kill as many people at his school as he could; he posted this threat on JuicyCampus.

The same concerns and criticisms have been leveled against a similar site, Collegiate ACB (for Collegiate Anonymous Confession Board). Created as College ACB in early 2008 by two university graduate students who are no longer connected with the site, Collegiate ACB allows students from more than five hundred colleges to post comments to and about fellow students. However, in response to complaints about hate speech, the site added a button that would allow users to report offensive posts, and if these reports prove justified the site will remove the posts. Nonetheless, there are still many hateful posts on the site because the cyberbullies who use it see nothing wrong with other cyberbullies' posts.

Shameless Behavior

Indeed, many cyberbullies see nothing wrong with posting such messages and show no remorse over their victims' pain. Some are so disconnected emotionally from their victims that they do

Cyberbullying Turns Dangerous

In some cases cyberbullying can lead to an offline physical assault. This was the case with Nafeesa Onque of New Jersey, whose problems with cyberbullying began in 2008 when she was fourteen years old. At that time, someone created a fake Myspace page that seemed like it belonged to her, then began using it to threaten people. Onque's mother was able to get Myspace to shut down the page. But the following year the bully created a fake Facebook page that looked like it belonged to Onque and used it to make Onque seem sexually promiscuous and to send vile messages to Onque's friends, many of whom then contacted Onque demanding to know why she had become so hateful. This time her mother was not able to get the page taken down, and neither school authorities nor police could help her—until in March 2010 when the imposter used the fake page to challenge another teenage girl to a fight. This girl subsequently attacked Onque, which led an officer with a state police unit specializing in digital crimes to track down the cyberbully. It turned out to be a girl at school jealous of Onque's popularity.

not even feel sorry when they push someone to commit suicide. One of the most prominent examples of such shamelessness is the case of fifteen-year-old Amanda Cummings of Staten Island, New York, who was bullied by a group of girls at school via text message and on Facebook. Cummings's cousin, twenty-year-old Ashley Gilman, later said, "No matter what she did, they picked on her. They made fun of her heels, her hair, her make-up—everything."[35]

The situation became worse after Cummings started dating a boy that the bullies' ringleader liked. Her tormenters called her names and threatened her with physical violence, and eventually the boy broke off their relationship. After he changed his Facebook status to show he was no longer dating Cummings, she was taunted over that as well.

For a long time she did nothing about the bullying for fear that reporting it would make it worse. After a few months, though, she finally showed her parents some of the abusive text messages. But by that point it was Christmas vacation so they could not discuss the problem with school authorities, and the next day Cummings received several abusive text messages. Feeling hopeless about her situation, she rushed out of her house upset, and shortly thereafter she threw herself in front of a city bus. In her pocket was a suicide note saying she could not live without the boy she had been dating.

While Cummings was lying unconscious in the hospital, the bullies continued to say horrible things about her via posts on her Facebook wall, ridiculing her for jumping in front of a bus and calling her sexually promiscuous. Then she died of her injuries, and still she was attacked on Facebook. But now it was from users of a website that promotes attacking suicide victims, 4Chan. This site is an image-based bulletin board where anyone can post comments and share images related to a variety of topics, but some of the site's users are cyberbullies who use it as a place to gather and discuss ways to attack others for sport.

After Cummings's friends and loved ones created a Facebook page in her memory, 4Chan cyberbullies posted a message calling on people to attack it. As a result, thousands visited the site to post hateful messages, images, videos, and pornography while mocking Cummings. They also harassed mourners who posted comments on the site, as well as a person who created a petition on the political website Change.org demanding that Facebook change its rules to prevent the desecration of memorial pages. Many people from Cummings's town decried 4Chan members' attacks.

One of them, Alyssa Vanderhoef, said of these cyberbullies, "They planned to make that page [their own] and bash on her death. They do it because they try to get their self-esteem up. It's from everyone all over the world. There's no control and stopping them. It just made me furious, because she didn't deserve anything that happened."[36] Another Staten Island resident upset by this cyberbullying, Matt O'Day, said, "I think it is wrong and disgusting that in this young girl's death she is still being bullied. I think it's worse that she is being bullied by people she didn't even know. A stupid website told its members to do it. Where do you draw the line of what is right or wrong?"[37]

Means of Bullying

Studies have shown that bullying via Facebook is not uncommon. In fact, according to a 2010 study by the Cyberbullying Research Center, 50.1 percent of cyberbullies bully via Facebook. One reason for the popularity of Facebook as a bullying tool is that social media sites provide people with the ability to create alias profiles, which means they can have anonymity when making their comments. Another reason is that social media provides bullies with access to personal information that makes the sharers of that information vulnerable to attack. That is, people posting on Facebook and similar sites often reveal things that they would never reveal in

Friends and family honor the life of seventeen-year-old Rehtaeh Parsons, who killed herself in April 2013. The Nova Scotia teenager was gang-raped and then subjected to horrific bullying after perpetrators posted a photo of the rape on social media sites.

a face-to-face conversation because of the same disinhibition effect that emboldens bullies.

The 2010 Cyberbullying Research Center study also found that 50.8 percent of cyberbullies bullied while using the Internet for schoolwork, and 83 percent of cyberbullies bullied via cell phone. Bullying via cell phone most often involves sending hurtful text messages, but cell phones can be used to take and/or send hurtful photos as well. Such was the case with the cyberbullying of seventeen-year-old Rehtaeh Parsons of Nova Scotia, who committed suicide in April 2013.

In November 2011 Parsons was gang-raped by four teenage boys at a party where she had been drinking. During this rape, one of the boys used his cell phone to take a picture of her that made it look like she could have been a willing participant in the sex. Shortly thereafter he shared the photo with classmates and posted it on Facebook and other social media sites. As a result, Parsons received numerous text and Facebook messages from people calling her horrible names and/or saying they wanted to have sex with her too.

When Parsons reported the rape and subsequent harassment to the Royal Canadian Mounted Police (RCMP), they did not take the cyberbullying seriously, and after a yearlong investigation into the rape they said they could find no evidence that the sex was anything but consensual. School officials also did nothing to help her end the cyberbullying, which went on for months. With no hope of seeing her tormentors punished, on April 4, 2013, Parsons hanged herself. She died in the hospital three days later, having never regained consciousness.

Criminal Activity

After her daughter's death, Parsons's mother railed on Facebook against the boys who had ruined her life and the life of her daughter and demanded justice. Meanwhile, her father posted an open letter to the RCMP on his blog, criticizing them for refusing to take either the rape accusations or the cyberbullying seriously even though they had photographic evidence of what had taken place. Of the boys' rape photo he said, "They posted it on their Facebook walls. They emailed it to God knows who. They shared it with the world as if it was a funny animation. How is it possible for someone to leave a digital trail like that yet the RCMP don't have evidence of a crime?"[38]

By this time the story had gained international attention, and the outcry that resulted from these parents' posts was huge. The public demanded that the RCMP take action, and to help spur them on, a computer hacker group called Anonymous vowed to find enough evidence to prove that the boys had committed rape. It took them only two hours to do so, because their vow brought a flood of e-mails and texts from people to whom the boys had bragged about what they had done. Consequently, charges were filed in August 2013 against the boy who was in the picture with Parsons and the boy who took the picture—not for rape but for distributing pornography (the rape picture) online.

Just prior to these charges being filed, Canadian prime minister Stephen Harper said, "I think we've got to stop just using just the term *bullying* to describe some of these things. Bullying to me has a connotation of kids misbehaving. What we are dealing with in some of these circumstances is simply criminal activity. It is youth criminal activity. It is violent criminal activity. It is sexual criminal activity, and it is often Internet criminal activity."[39]

But while this might be true, cyberbullying experts say that it is important to go beyond labels in order to examine the reasons why some people are so willing to hurt others so viciously and without remorse. They continue to call for more research into cyberbullies' psyches even as they applaud actions taken to respond more harshly to cyberbullying. Gaining an understanding of how bullies think is important, they say, but so too is making it clear to young people that cyberbullying is always wrong.

"I think we've got to stop just using just the term bullying to describe some of these things. Bullying to me has a connotation of kids misbehaving. What we are dealing with in some of these circumstances is simply criminal activity."[39]

— Canadian prime minister Stephen Harper.

Facts

- Studies have shown that whereas teachers say they intervene in bullying incidents most of the time, students say that teachers rarely intervene.

- According to the antibullying organization DoSomething.org, 90 percent of teens who have seen social media bullying admit they ignored it, although 84 percent said they have seen others online tell cyberbullies to stop.

- The website Bullying Statistics reports that one in five teens will become a victim of a text bully.

- According to the *Hartford County Examiner* in 2010, 71 percent of teen girls and 67 percent of teen boys who have sent or posted sexually suggestive content did so in order to share that content with a boyfriend or girlfriend; experts say most never considered that it might be maliciously shared with others after a breakup.

- The National Crime Prevention Council reports that cyberbullying is more common among females than males and most prevalent among fifteen- and sixteen-year-olds.

How Does Cyberbullying Affect Victims?

The impact of cyberbullying on victims can range from upsetting to devastating, depending on how extreme the bullying is. However, the most extreme cases best illustrate just how profoundly cyberbullying can ruin a person's life. When law enforcement officers in Maine are asked to name such a case, most immediately point to the cyberbullying that fifteen-year-old Alexis Henkel endured in Orono, Maine, in 2012. Police sergeant Keith Emery says, "I've handled harassment calls for 24 years and have never seen threats as violent, disgusting and vulgar as these. They started out telling the girl she was ugly, a whore, slut, et cetera. . . . Just very vulgar and horrific threats. There were dozens of these types of messages."[40]

The first of these messages appeared in late September 2012 on a blog that Henkel had on a site called Tumblr. By the following month the anonymous poster had begun to threaten her with violence. One such message read: "Ready for tomorrow night? I'd learn to sleep with your eyes open if I were you. I'm dulling my knife right now so when I stab you in the face, gut and legs it'll be painful as possible." Another said: "Your face is like a baby seal. Fat, furry and just asking to be clubbed to death."[41] Other messages spoke of dismembering her, stalking her, or raping her. In one message the poster threatened to haunt Henkel forever and eventually hurt any children she might have.

Sexual Cyberbullying

One of the fastest-growing types of cyberbullying is sexual cyberbullying. Also called slut shaming, this involves shaming girls online for behaving in sexually promiscuous ways, even when the victim is not actually engaging in this behavior. Sexual cyberbullying often involves posting sexually explicit photos and/or videos of the victim, perhaps taken by guests at a party where the girl was drunk or by a guy who has secretly recorded his own sexual activities with the victim out of a desire to brag about it later. When such images are shared by cell phone instead of via online posts the practice is commonly known as sexting, for sexual texting. However, sexting often involves the person shown in the photo being the one to send the photo. In a 2012 study by the University of Utah of youths ages fourteen to eighteen, nearly 20 percent said they had sexted a sexually explicit image of themselves, typically to a boyfriend or girlfriend.

Perhaps even more disturbing was the fact that some of the messages made Henkel think that the poster knew her personally and might possibly know exactly where she lived. For example, she was referred to by her common nickname, Lexi, rather than Alexis, and the poster was clearly familiar with her school. Consequently, when the poster began threatening to show up at her house to hurt her, Henkel took these threats seriously, and her parents reported them to police. Her father later said, "We really didn't know how to take it at first, how seriously to take it, but as it was going on [and we were] reading those messages, it felt like somebody [who] writes that would be so disturbed you don't know what else they would do. . . . We really became worried about her [Lexi's] well-being and her safety. There were days we left home, we went somewhere else, for the simple reason that somebody was threatening to come over to the house and shoot at the house."[42]

Identifying the Bully

In cooperation with police, Henkel's parents kept the Tumblr account open so that the anonymous poster could continue making threats. The police hoped that this would give them more clues as to the poster's identity. Meanwhile, they worked to determine the source of the posts and soon discovered that nearly all had come from a computer at Henkel's school. Her parents decided to keep her home from school, and with the agreement of police they shut down the Henkel's Tumblr account. Henkel's attacker started sending threatening text messages anonymously to Henkel's cell phone.

Police were then able to identify the sender as sixteen-year-old May Callahan, a former classmate of Henkel's who thought Henkel had been flirting with her boyfriend. They charged the offender with felony terrorizing and harassment by electronic communication—felonies instead of misdemeanors because the threats had sometimes made Henkel's family flee their home in fear. In March 2013 Callahan pleaded guilty to one count of felony terrorizing and one count of misdemeanor harassment (reduced from a felony as part of her plea agreement) and received a suspended sentence with no jail time or fines.

At the sentencing hearing, Henkel and her parents were each allowed to make victim statements. Henkel told of how she had to miss school and school activities, such as homecoming, and eventually had to transfer schools because other students from her school also harassed her online after Callahan started tormenting her. Henkel's father talked about the fear his family had experienced and the nightmares that his daughter had and was still having as a result of her trauma. He also said, "For all we knew, it could have been anybody. . . . It was hard for me to believe a young girl could spew such mean and vile things like you did. What you wrote made me, as an adult, blush. You wrote things no young person—or anybody, for that matter—should know about. The sick ways you imagined killing my daughter still send chills down my back. . . . I'm glad you could be stopped before you could actually . . . [hurt] Alexis. I do believe you and some of your friends would have done that."[43]

In addition, Henkel's father expressed extreme disappointment over the plea bargain that had spared Callahan any meaningful punishment. She simply had to stay away from the Henkels, attend school regularly, and stay out of trouble. But in a tearful statement at the hearing, Callahan insisted that while she was sorry for what she had done, she was suffering too. She said, "This has impacted many people, mostly the victim. It has also impacted me. I admit to what I've done. To be honest, I just would like my life back."[44]

Suicidal Thoughts

But as Henkel's mother angrily pointed out, Callahan's actions almost made Henkel lose her life entirely. She explained, "My daughter thought of taking her own life and I thank God every day for the relationship that I have with my daughter. For days and weeks I slept with my daughter in my arms to make sure that she was breathing. All over jealousy over nothing, you destroyed her life, you destroyed her high school years and you're a coward. You couldn't even post in your own name. You had to post anonymously."[45]

"You destroyed her life, you destroyed her high school years and you're a coward. You couldn't even post in your own name. You had to post anonymously."[45]

— Judy Henkel on the cyberbully who tormented her daughter.

Thoughts of suicide are becoming an increasingly common response to severe cases of cyberbullying. Studies have shown that young people who have been technobullied (bullied via some form of technology) are twice as likely to have sought out a mental health professional for treatment. According to the Cyberbullying Research Center, a cyberbullying victim is 1.9 times more likely to attempt suicide than nonvictims. Another study by Yale University shows that victims of any kind of bullying are 2 to 9 times more likely to consider suicide than nonvictims.

Many victims who have had suicidal thoughts are reluctant to speak of them. However, a few are willing to come forward to share their feelings so that nonvictims can understand the kind of despair that cyberbullying can create. For example, in a May 2013 article titled "I Was Cyberbullied" for the digital magazine *Thought Catalog*, therapist Kelsey Kangos writes of her own experiences as a victim of cyberbullying when she was in middle school. Her torment began simply

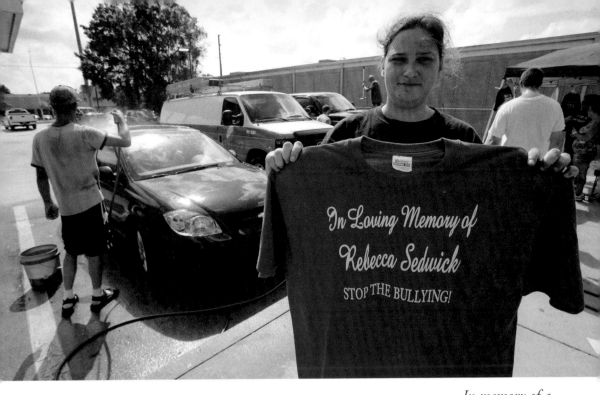

because classmates suddenly decided that her arms were too hairy. As a result, kids started calling her names like "gorilla" at school and kept trying to trip her as she walked down the halls. Then the face-to-face bullying turned into cyberbullying. She reports:

> Screen names started popping up on AOL Instant Messenger that were created for the sole purpose of harassment. "kelseyISaGORILLA", "kelseyisacrybaby", "shaveHAIRY", and countless others. These screen names would come up saying horrible things about my weight, about how I had no friends, and asking why I didn't just "do the rest of the world a favor" and shave my arms? It escalated to such an extreme that they told me they would be happy if I would just kill myself. . . . An extensive website was created for the sole purpose of making fun of me, with my picture being uploaded and put onto a gorilla's body, with fake journal entries supposedly written by me—one even claiming I said I was going to bring a gun to school, a "spotted" section logging my whereabouts . . . and polls about whether I should shave, and whether I should kill myself.[46]

Eventually Kangos internalized these messages, thinking she really should kill herself. She says, "Things got so bad that I legitimately contemplated suicide. Everything I knew, my entire world, was complete misery."[47]

Taking Things Seriously

Finally Kangos told her mother and her mother's boyfriend Thom what had been happening, and Thom confronted the parents of the boy who had created the website. As a result the website was shut down, but Kangos's school did nothing to help her with the remainder of the bullying. She says, "I pleaded with our assistant principal that action should be taken, and none ever was. I tried to handle it on my own before it became too much to bear. Luckily, I chose to involve my parents instead of [doing] something drastic against myself." She criticizes adults who fail to take bullying seriously, saying, "Bullying is something that is so accepted in our society as a product of that age group, but when are we going to wake up and realize the devastating toll it is taking on our youth?"[48]

Others have questioned whether cyberbullying really does take a devastating toll. Specifically, some experts say that people are too quick to assume that a suicide that follows months of cyberbullying is necessarily the result of the cyberbullying. One such expert is guidance counselor Chuck Saufler, co-coordinator of the Maine Project Against Bullying. He points out that in regard to the CDC's research indicating that suicide is the third leading cause of death for young people, this statistic was the same prior to the creation of social media.

He also notes that no research has proved a causal relationship between cyberbullying and suicidal thoughts or behavior, only a correlational one. That is, cyberbullying and suicidal thoughts or behavior might have a connection to one another, but there is no proof that one directly causes the other. Saufler argues, "Adolescent suicide is not caused by any one factor, but by a combination of them. The CDC lists over 30 'risk factors' known to contribute

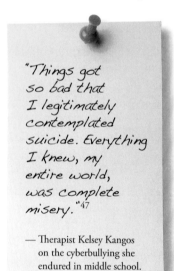

"Things got so bad that I legitimately contemplated suicide. Everything I knew, my entire world, was complete misery."[47]

— Therapist Kelsey Kangos on the cyberbullying she endured in middle school.

to adolescent suicide. No single one in isolation has proven to have a causal connection to suicide rates, but the cumulative effects of multiple risk factors have been shown to increase the potential for a suicide attempt by an individual." Therefore, he argues, "we need to push the 'pause button' when we hear the media say 'cyberbullying drove someone to suicide.'"[49]

Media Influence

Paul Butler, a former federal prosecutor who is now a professor at the George Washington University Law School, holds a similar view. He also argues that suicide is a much rarer response to bullying than the media would make it seem. He says, "Of the millions of children who suffer bullying, few take their own lives. Bullies 'cause' suicides in the same way that a man 'causes' the suicide of a lover he spurns."[50]

Saufler suggests that talking about suicide in relation to cyberbullying might also be causing an increase in suicides. He explains, "There is a real danger in the media overexposure of the idea that suicide is an answer to victimization. We know that media attention to youth suicides increases copycat attempts by other adolescents. As my colleague, Stan Davis says, 'Over predicting harm causes more harm.' As long as the national media outlets and websites repeatedly hype cyberbullying as causing these tragedies, the harm caused will increase."[51]

"Adolescent suicide is not caused by any one factor, but by a combination of them."[49]

— Chuck Saufler, co-coordinator of the Maine Project Against Bullying.

Depression and Anxiety

One of the risk factors mentioned by the CDC is depression, which studies show is associated with more than 75 percent of suicides. Some experts say that since cyberbullying appears to cause depression and depression often seems to cause suicide, it is logical to assume that cyberbullying and suicidal thoughts and behaviors do have a causal relationship. Saufler disagrees with this, pointing out that depression can be the result of any one or more of a number of factors, such as a psychological tendency toward depression, that can predate or have nothing to do with the cyberbullying.

However, many victims of cyberbullying talk about the overwhelming depression they experienced because of their tormentors. As one fourteen-year-old girl from Illinois told researchers with the Cyberbullying Research Center about how it felt to be cyberbullied, "It makes me depressed a lot. It affected me for about 3–4 years. I hated being [cyber]bullied. I would come home and just cry. It really hurt."[52] Similarly, a twelve-year-old girl from Massachusetts told the researchers, "It lowers my self-esteem. It makes me feel really crappy. It makes me walk around the rest of the day feeling worthless, like no one cares. It makes me very, very depressed."[53]

People who have been cyberbullied—whether young people or adults—can experience not only depression but anxiety, loneliness, unhappiness, self-pity, insecurity, and insomnia. They can also feel embarrassed, helpless, fearful, frustrated, and/or angry. However, studies by the Cyberbullying Research Center have found that whereas elementary, middle, and high school victims all feel depression, sadness, and frustration to roughly the same degree, significantly more elementary school victims than middle and high school victims experience sadness.

Cyberbullying can also make victims feel psychologically battered because it can seem relentless. John Carr explains, "When I was a kid, playground bullying stopped when the bell rang and you went back inside or went home," he says. "With cyber-bullying it is 24/7, 365 days a year. There is no escape."[54] In addition, Robin M. Kowalski reports that anonymity amplifies the harm caused to the victim. She says, "The psychological ramifications of not knowing who's attacking you can be maddening. The bully could be your best friend, a sibling or half the school."[55]

Altered Behavior

In addition to affecting emotions, cyberbullying can affect victims' behavior. They might avoid going to school—or to work, in the case of adults cyberbullied while on the job. They might also alter their habits in regard to Internet use, either to avoid encountering

> "Of the millions of children who suffer bullying, few take their own lives. Bullies 'cause' suicides in the same way that a man 'causes' the suicide of a lover he spurns."[50]
>
> — Paul Butler, a former federal prosecutor and a professor at the George Washington University Law School.

more cyberbullying or to obsessively monitor websites and e-mail to see whether new accusations or threats have appeared.

Victims experiencing fear typically alter their behavior the most, especially if they become genuinely worried about their physical safety. Sameer Hinduja and Justin W. Patchin report:

> At some point, victims may become preoccupied with plotting ways to avoid certain peers while instant messaging or chatting with their friends on the Internet. Indeed, victims might be consumed with avoiding certain cyberbullies whom they actually know in person—either at school,

Severe depression, no matter what a person's age, is considered a risk factor for suicide. Many factors contribute to severe depression; cyberbullying might be one factor, but there are also many others.

at the bus stop, or in their neighborhood. Whichever the case, when youths are constantly surveilling the landscape of cyberspace or real space to guard against problematic interpersonal encounters, their ability to focus on academics, family matters and responsibilities, and prosocial choices is compromised to some extent.[56]

Taking Action

Other victims adopt a different sort of behavior in response to cyberbullying: They take action to stop the bullying. This is particularly true with adult victims, who are more likely to channel their anger and frustration into pursing their tormentors with the aim of seeing them punished. An example of this is the case of Susan Arnout Smith, a writer from San Diego.

In 2011 a colleague told Smith that there was a Facebook page under her name that was "disturbing." When Smith checked it out, she was mortified. She says, "I saw my face. It was a photo taken off one of my websites. I saw my name. The persona they had created, using my name, my face, was pornographic, trolling for sex. . . . I sat stunned."[57] Fearing this would ruin her reputation, she tried to get Facebook to remove the page, with no success. She then went to the police, who told her that unless her online problem involved stalking or a significant monetary loss, they could not help her.

As time passed, her embarrassment turned to feelings of powerlessness, then anger. "A slow rage burned in my heart," she says. This anger was fueled by continuing concerns about her career, which made it difficult for her to sleep each night. She explains, "I had built my reputation brick by brick over decades, one project at a time, only to discover that out there in cyberspace, my life and reputation had been shredded."[58] After more than month of seething, she finally decided to take control of her situation and embarked on a mission to locate the person who had created the page.

Smith did this by examining the comments left not only on the fake page but on the pages of the twenty-two Facebook friends

"The psychological ramifications of not knowing who's attacking you can be maddening. The bully could be your best friend, a sibling or half the school."[55]

— South Carolina psychologist Robin M. Kowalski, coauthor of the book *Cyberbullying: Bullying in the Digital Age.*

A Cyberbullying Victim Attacks the Bully

Sometimes the victim of cyberbullying can become upset enough to track down the bully with the intent to do bodily harm. For example, in March 2010 Wayne Treacy of Florida, then fifteen years old, grew angry while exchanging texts with fifteen-year-old Josie Ratley, a friend of his thirteen-year-old girlfriend, Kayla Manson. He had never met Ratley, but Ratley had gotten his cell phone number when Manson used Ratley's phone to text him. Believing Treacy was too old for Manson, Ratley texted him and told him to leave her friend alone. An argument via text ensued, during which Ratley called Treacy a rapist, threatened him with physical violence, and hurled insults at him. She also brought up Treacy's older brother, who had recently committed suicide by hanging himself from a tree, and told Treacy to go visit his dead brother. Enraged, he ended the call, declared he wanted to kill Ratley, went to his girlfriend, and demanded that she point Ratley out. Once Manson did this, Treacy beat Ratley into a coma, and when she recovered days later she was left brain damaged. In October 2012 he was sentenced to twenty years in prison for his crime.

of whomever had created the page. By following various threads she learned as much as she could about all of these people and eventually she figured out exactly where they lived and who was behind the creation of the Facebook page. Her cyberbullies attended two different schools in another country where there were laws against what they had done.

Shaming the Bully

Smith's first instinct was to publicly shame and ruin the boys who had hurt her, perhaps by bringing them to the attention of law enforcement and/or filing a lawsuit against them. But as she investigated the boys further she discovered that they were promising students who apparently had not otherwise been in trouble. So instead she contacted their school principals and told them what was going on.

One of the principals managed to get Facebook to shut down the page, but neither principal could figure out why the boys had selected Smith's name to use for their fake page. Smith believes she knows why: "My guess? I wasn't real to them. I was a bouncy toy, a name, a face, pulled at random off the Net. Something they tossed into the air and batted around for a couple of months before they lost interest and moved on. That, for me, is the scariest part."[59] Still, Smith decided never to make their names public, although she did extract a promise from the principals to tell the boys' parents exactly what they had done.

Unfortunately, the difficulties that Smith experienced prior to taking matters into her own hands are common. Far too often, law enforcement officers do not take cyberbullying seriously unless the victim has experienced serious, perhaps life-threatening harm. Moreover, Facebook and other social media sites have often been criticized for their inaction when it comes to removing content related to cyberbullying. Consequently, many people have called for tougher laws and policies that will compel others to help victims end their torment if, unlike Smith, they are unable to vanquish the cyberbullies on their own.

Facts

- The CDC reports that suicide is the third leading cause of death among fifteen- to twenty-four-year-olds.

- A study by psychologist Dan Olweus of the University of Bergen in Norway suggests a connection between being victimized in grades 6 and 9 and experiencing greater depression and lower self-esteem at age twenty-three.

- In examining forty-one cases of suicides related to cyberbullying, John C. LeBlanc, a professor at Dalhousie University in Halifax, Nova Scotia, found that social networking sites were used by the cyberbullies in 48 percent of these cases while messaging (text, pictures, or video) was used in 25 percent of the cases.

- According to DoSomething.org, an antibullying organization, 70 percent of students report having frequently seen bullying online.

- A survey of young people by the Associated Press and MTV in 2011 found that 34 percent said they were either very or somewhat likely to retaliate against someone who had cyberbullied them.

CHAPTER FOUR

How Effective Are Cyberbullying Laws?

L awmakers disagree on how best to approach the problem of cyberbullying. Consequently, laws created with the intent of preventing and punishing cyberbullies vary greatly from country to country and, within the United States, from state to state. This means that when it comes to charging a cyberbully with a crime, whether the charge is a felony or a misdemeanor—or whether it is considered a crime at all—depends on where the events took place.

US Laws

In the United States as of July 2013 forty-seven states have an antibullying law that specifically includes electronic harassment as a form of bullying. However, only eighteen of these states specifically mention cyberbullying in their laws. (Electronic harassment involves serious threats made via an electronic device, whereas cyberbullying can involve not only major and minor threats but embarrassing, cruel, or otherwise negative posts, photos, e-mails, and text messages.)

In addition, only twelve states include criminal sanctions in their bullying laws, and some states have less severe sentences for those convicted of such crimes than others. For example, in Tennessee certain instances of cyber harassment bring a misdemeanor charge that can result in a year in prison and a $2,500 fine. In Missouri a case of cyberbullying is charged as a misdemeanor unless it was committed by someone age twenty-one or older against someone age seventeen or younger, in which case the crime is charged as a type of felony with a sentence of up to four years in jail.

States that have an antibullying law but do not have criminal sanctions leave it to schools to deal with cyberbullies. Specifically, forty-nine states require schools to have a policy in place to deal with bullying and mandate that school officials take immediate action to stop it. But only eleven of these states include bullying that takes place off campus as well as at school. Moreover, while forty-four of these states mandate school sanctions, such as suspensions or transferring the bully to an alternative school, most leave punishment up to school administrators.

Other Ways to Prosecute

At least five other states are also considering making cyberbullying a criminal offense, and there have been proposals to make it a crime at the federal level as well. But some experts do not believe such laws are necessary. This is because some of the most serious aspects of a cyberbullying incident, such as stalking and assault, can be prosecuted under existing state and/or federal laws.

A prominent example of this is the case of Matthew Bean, who in January 2011, at the age of twenty, was sentenced in US district court to forty-five days in prison, five years' probation, and $2,000 in fines. Two years earlier, Bean had come across sexually explicit photos of a boy on a website and posted them on his own web page, then invited comments. (The boy had posted the photos himself when he was twelve or thirteen, but they were on his own page on a website that was simply for posting photos.) Bean's invitation to comment led to brutal remarks that included a hope that the boy would kill himself after seeing the remarks.

To ensure that the boy was aware of what was going on, Bean pretended to be a concerned parent and forwarded the photos to teachers and administrators at the boy's private school in Philadelphia, Pennsylvania. The school then contacted law enforcement,

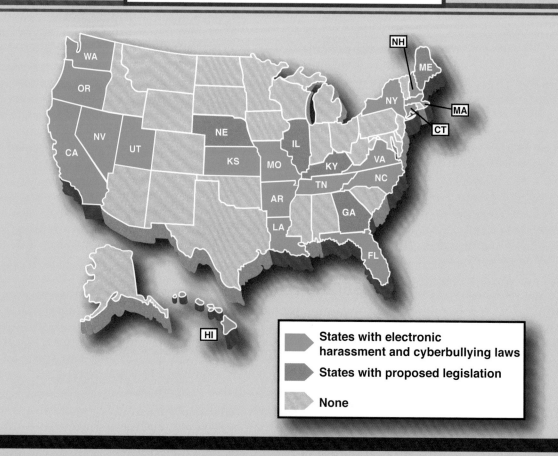

States with Cyberbullying Laws

NH
ME
NY
MA
CT
WA
OR
NV
CA
UT
NE
IL
KS
MO
KY
VA
TN
NC
AR
GA
LA
FL
HI

States with electronic harassment and cyberbullying laws

States with proposed legislation

None

Source: Cyberbullying Research Center, "State Cyberbullying Laws." July 2013. www.cyberbullying.us

and the FBI became involved because it is a federal offense to share or otherwise exploit sexually explicit images of anyone under the age of eighteen. Consequently, after the FBI discovered Bean's identity and arrested him, they were able to charge him with fifteen felony counts related to the distribution of pornography involving a minor—but not with cyberbullying, since it is not a federal crime.

Civil Suits

In many cyberbullying cases, however, there is no chargeable crime involved. For example, some harassment laws apply only if an actionable threat (a threat that can actually be carried out) has been made while the perpetrator and the victim are in direct communication with one another. Under such laws, even if a threat is serious and it seems that the bully would be able to carry out the threat, if it has been posted on a website rather than communicated via e-mail, phone, or in person, it would not be a prosecutable offense.

Because victims cannot always depend on law enforcement to help them end online harassment, some have found another way to get their tormentors into court: filing a civil suit against them. This action was taken by fourteen-year-old Alex Boston of Ken-

Cyberbullying via Death Photo

In one of the worst cases of cyberbullying involving a grieving family, cyberbullies circulated photos of a dead teenager online and created a fake Myspace page that at first appeared to be a tribute to the girl but actually led visitors to the death photos. The teenager was eighteen-year-old Nikki Catsouras, who died in a car crash on a toll road in Orange County, California, in October 2006. The following month two dispatchers with the California Highway Patrol (CHP) put graphic photos of her remains on the Internet. These images quickly went viral, and cyberbullies began making vile remarks about the girl and her family. Some said the girl deserved to die, others that she had been drunk or on drugs while driving, and they accused her mother and father of being horrible parents. The Catsouras family turned to an online reputation management company to try to get the photos removed from the Internet, but because they were in so many places this cost them thousands of dollars. In July 2007 the family sued the CHP for allowing the images to go public, and in January 2012 the CHP settled the lawsuit by agreeing to pay the family $2.37 million.

nesaw, Georgia, and her parents after she was bullied on Facebook by classmates.

Georgia has an antibullying law, but it addresses only electronic harassment, not cyberbullying, and it does not treat electronic harassment as a criminal act. Instead it only mandates that school sanctions be imposed against cyberbullies, and only if their cyberbullying takes place on school grounds. Therefore, when Boston reported her bullying to police in May 2011, they said they could not help her. The same was true of officials at Boston's middle school, who noted that Facebook is an off-campus activity. Boston then complained to Facebook, which failed to remove the offending material from its site.

This material was a fake account under her name, with a fake profile, a photograph of her that had been altered to make her face look unattractive, and remarks that made Boston seem to be a racist and a sexually promiscuous drug user. The profile prompted other people to make hateful comments about her, and she found the experience so upsetting that she refused to stop trying to remedy the situation. Finally in April 2012, after determining that the account had been set up by two of her classmates, she and her parents filed a lawsuit against them and their parents. The grounds of the lawsuit were libel, defamation of character, and the intentional infliction of emotional distress, and the cyberbullies' parents were included in the suit because they had paid for their teens' Internet access and had failed to supervise their online activities. (As of August 2013 the case had apparently not yet been resolved, but upon being notified of the lawsuit Facebook shut down the offensive account.)

Tracking Down Perpetrators

In commenting on Boston's lawsuit, attorney and cybersafety expert Parry Aftab said that she would not be surprised if many other families took the same approach in trying to combat cyberbullying. The criminal justice system is not equipped to deal with such problems, she says, and adds, "A lot of prosecutors just don't have the energy to prosecute 13-year-olds for being mean. Parents are

> "A lot of prosecutors just don't have the energy to prosecute 13-year-olds for being mean."[60]
>
> — Attorney and cybersafety expert Parry Aftab.

Free Speech

While some Americans are pushing for more cyberbullying laws, others argue that such laws would violate the First Amendment of the US Constitution, which guarantees the right to free speech. There are exceptions under this law; perhaps the best-known example is one that does not allow people to yell "Fire!" in a crowded theater as a prank because in the ensuing panic people could be trampled. Consequently, New York State senator Jeffrey D. Klein, who advocates stricter punishments for cyberbullies, says, "The Constitution is very clear. Free speech ends when you harm someone else. Words can kill."

Nonetheless, in response to legal challenges to school suspensions brought on by cyberbullying, some courts have sided with the cyberbully on the grounds that their right to free speech has been violated. For example, in November 2009 a US District Court found that it was wrong for a school to suspend a girl for two days because she posted a video on YouTube of a group of girls speaking horribly about a classmate. The court felt that offensive speech is not the same as harmful speech, noting that the video did nothing to disrupt on-campus school activities.

Quoted in Elbert Chu, "Should Cyberbullying Be a Crime?," WNYC, April 27, 2012. www.wnyc.org.

all feeling very frustrated, and they just don't know what to do."[60] Indeed, in August 2013 Nova Scotia enacted a law that allows cyberbullying victims to hold the parents of the bullies liable for damages if those bullies are minors.

But before a cyberbully can be sued in civil court or tried in criminal court, his or her identity must be uncovered. In many cases this can be accomplished by finding out the bully's Internet protocol (IP) address, a unique string of numbers identifying each computer connected to the Internet. Police must obtain a subpoena to compel an Internet provider to provide the IP address of the computer from which a remark or threat was transmitted on-line, but when this happens—unless the computer is being shared by many users, as in a school computer lab—it is usually easy to track down the offender. Consequently, as a Colorado detective said after catching a fifteen-year-old cyberbully this way, "While people may believe they are anonymous, it is still possible to trace IP addresses to determine who 'anonymous' really is."[61]

But in other cases cyberbullies take more pains to hide their tracks. As a result, police might not want to devote resources to the search, especially if the bullies' actions are minor in their eyes or it is doubtful that criminal charges can be filed. This leaves victims or their parents to try to track down the culprits. Those who have no idea how to do this might turn to cybersecurity experts for help.

In May 2013 the *Daily Telegraph* reported that some of these experts make as much as $800 a day helping parents track down anonymous cyberbullies. One such private investigator, Jason King, says that most of his income now comes from uncovering the identities of Facebook bullies. He states, "I get three calls a day about it, and the youngest I've had is about 11–12. And I take on 50 per cent of them." He explains that sometimes a parent comes to him suspecting the cyberbully's identity and asking him to prove that suspicion, while others have no idea who it might be. He adds, "I've also done a fair few hate pages as well, with families who are grieving contacting me to determine who has set up a Facebook site targeting them. Most of them are unknown to the family; they do it because they can."[62]

King further reports that once he tracks down the perpetrator, he lets the family decide what to do with that information, although, depending on the nature of the cyberbullying, he might suggest they turn it over to school officials or police. Nina Hobson, director of an investigations group called Meridian Services, says she takes a similar approach. However, on some occasions she confronts the cyberbully directly to warn that if the bullying does not stop she will reveal the information to school authorities, police, or parents.

"Few can agree on the point when cyberbullying behavior crosses the threshold at which the criminal or civil law is implicated."[68]

— Sameer Hinduja and Justin W. Patchin of the Cyberbullying Research Center.

Other Targets

By this time, though, most victims will have already suffered greatly. Consequently, some experts have suggested passing laws that will make it much more difficult for cyberbullies to launch an attack. Specifically, these experts want to target the websites that give cyberbullies a place to do their bullying.

In Italy lawmakers are already targeting social media sites that have failed to act quickly to delete bullying content. In 2010 three Google Italia executives were given suspended jail terms for ignoring requests to remove a video of teens bullying a handicapped boy, posted in 2006. The prosecutors in this case argued that these men were criminally liable because of their inaction.

Italian prosecutors have also considered going after Facebook in regard to the January 2013 suicide of Carolina Picchio, a fourteen-year-old from Novara, Italy, who jumped out of a fourth-floor window after being cyberbullied on the social media site. Right before she jumped she updated her Facebook status with a note reading, "Forgive me if I'm not strong. I cannot take it any longer."[63]

> "If you hurt a 15-year-old's feelings really badly, do you go to jail for that?"[69]
>
> — Hanni Fakhoury of the Electronic Freedom Foundation.

The cyberbullying that Picchio endured was associated with a video that was being circulated by her ex-boyfriend and his friends. It showed Picchio apparently drunk and behaving in a sexually suggestive manner. The boys responsible for the video had also been insulting and threatening her via text messages and Facebook. On the day of her suicide she received twenty-six hundred obscene messages through Whatsapp, a mobile messaging app for phones.

After her death prosecutors filed criminal charges against eight boys, including Picchio's ex-boyfriend, who were between the ages of thirteen and seventeen. Their crimes were distributing child pornography over the Internet and driving someone to commit suicide. In May 2013 investigators also began trying to determine whether Picchio had tried to get Facebook to remove the offending material, in which case prosecutors would consider filing criminal charges against company executives as well.

Overworked, Underpaid

Italy's parents' association, Moige, supports efforts to hold Facebook responsible for Picchio's death. Moige's president, Maria Rita Munizzi, says, "It is bad that a corporation like Facebook does not carry a watch on virtual places, which seem to have become the preferred means of pedophiles and bullies. We are angry and worried about the silence and indifference shown by those who manage these powerful means of communication, who continue to function without an adequate policy to protect minors."[64]

However, policies and laws are two different things, and some

Some large companies hire outside businesses to review comments made on their websites and remove any that are deemed inappropriate. The British social network Bebo is among those companies that outsource these moderator jobs, as they are known.

people say it is wrong to hold the owners of a website criminally responsible for the actions of its users. They point out that when someone makes a complaint about content, it is not typically a company executive who first considers the complaint but a lower-level worker. Moreover, these workers might be employed by a different company, perhaps located in a foreign country where wages are low. Adam Levin, owner of British social network Bebo, says it is not uncommon for large companies to outsource moderator jobs in this way. (A moderator is someone tasked with reviewing comments made on a site and removing any inappropriate ones and/or preventing such comments from being seen by the public in the first place.) He says that Bebo outsources moderator jobs, and it is even more necessary for Facebook to do so because "Facebook has so much content flowing into its system every day that it needs hundreds of people moderating all the images and posts which are flagged. That type of workforce is best outsourced for speed, scale and cost."[65]

As of July 2013 Facebook had 699 million daily active users worldwide who shared an estimated 4 billion pieces of content per day. Levin estimates the company employs only eight hundred to one thousand moderators to review content, at wages that might be as low as one dollar an hour. These moderators are provided with guidelines on what is and is not acceptable to share on the site, and in many cases it is easy for them to decide that certain remarks or images should be removed. Other times it is not as obvious.

But when certain material is reported by Facebook users as objectionable, the moderator must make a decision on how to proceed, and that decision affects whether anyone higher up in the company will view the material. As Emma Barnett and Iain Hollingshead of England's *Telegraph* explain: "Once something is reported by a user, the moderator sitting at his computer in Morocco or Mexico has three options: delete it; ignore it; or escalate it, which refers it back to a Facebook employee in California (who will, if necessary, report it to the authorities). Moderators are told always to escalate specific

> "We don't think legislation is the best way to deal with cyber-bullying. When we take the opportunity to have kids talk to us and listen to us, we make more progress than the police."[71]
>
> — New York district attorney Cy Vance Jr.

threats—'I'm going to stab Lisa H at the frat party' is given as the charming example—but not generic, unlikely ones, such as 'I'm going to blow up the planet on New Year's Eve.'"[66]

Unfairly Targeted

Some people say it is ridiculous to expect that any site with so many users can effectively police its content. Others say that such sites certainly generate enough money to be able to hire enough workers to ensure that all complaints will be handled promptly and effectively. But there are also those who point out that even if websites are effectively policed it will not end cyberbullying, because there are so many other means of communication at the bullies' disposal.

In fact, some argue that laws and policies addressing specific types of Internet use are unfair. For example, Anna North of the online magazine *Jezebel* says that "cyberbullying laws could unfairly target bloggers" in the same way that libel laws "can leave some journalists afraid to criticize anyone."[67] In other words, because of cyberbullying laws, bloggers might become afraid to speak harshly of anyone or allow others commenting on their blog posts to do so even if the comments are justified and use inoffensive language. North also says there is a danger of overprosecution as the authorities seek to show that harassment is unacceptable.

Others have also worried about overprosecution because, as Sameer Hinduja and Justin W. Patchin point out, while "most can agree that certain forms of cyberbullying do not require formal (legal) intervention (e.g., minor teasing) . . . few can agree on the point when cyberbullying behavior crosses the threshold at which the criminal or civil law is implicated."[68] Or as Hanni Fakhoury, staff lawyer for the Electronic Freedom Foundation, says, "If you hurt a 15-year-old's feelings really badly, do you go to jail for that?"[69]

Bullying into Adulthood

Largely because determining where to draw the line is so difficult, Hinduja and Patchin have stated repeatedly that they do not want cyberbullying criminalized. But another reason they do not want it criminalized is that they do not believe this approach to dealing with cyberbullying works. Patchin explains, "We know from decades of research that teens are not deterred by threat of formal punishment. They are more likely to be deterred by relationships they care about within the schools and what their friends think."[70] Similarly, Cy Vance Jr., a New York district attorney, says, "We don't think legislation is the best way to deal with cyber-bullying. When we take the opportunity to have kids talk to us and listen to us, we make more progress than the police."[71]

But not all cyberbullies are children or teens. Adults can also cyberbully. In fact, experts say that cyberbullying is growing among women, especially on blogs and social media sites. Cheryl Dellasega, cyberbullying expert and author of *Mean Girls Grown Up*, reports, "It's been shocking to me to hear some of the ways in which women communicate online. Message boards get shut down. Sites get shut down. People drop off of sites. And it really becomes like a war, a cyber war, because they can't resolve it." She adds that this can be an extension of childhood behaviors, saying, "I certainly have run across women that learned as middle schoolers or high schoolers that intimidation and manipulation and humiliation were ways to get what they wanted."[72]

"It's been shocking to me to hear some of the ways in which women communicate online."[72]

— Cheryl Dellasega, author of *Mean Girls Grown Up*.

Other experts have also noted that bullying behavior can be carried from childhood into adulthood. However, this behavior does not necessarily rise to the level of a criminal offense. Consequently, some people believe that lawmakers need to find punishments for adult bullies that are the equivalent of school sanctions, such as requiring community service. But as with other kinds of cyberbullying, lawmakers cannot agree on what type of laws, if any, would be effective in dealing with the problem. In fact, as North notes, "Cyberbullying may be new, but bullying itself is one of the many ancient human evils we don't really know how to curtail."[73]

Facts

- According to Italy's postal police, who investigate Internet crimes, there have been fifty-four criminal complaints related to cyberbullying so far in 2013, compared with thirty such formal complaints in all of 2012.

- In Australia in August 2013 lawmakers proposed a law that would allow schools to be sued if they did not take steps to protect students from cyberbullying via wireless devices anywhere on school grounds.

- According to the website Bullying Statistics, fewer than one in five cyberbullying incidents are reported to law enforcement.

- Among young people surveyed in 2011 by the Associated Press and MTV, 29 percent worried that certain things they had shared via text messages or websites, particularly social media ones like Facebook and Myspace, would get them in trouble with police.

- According to a 2010 survey by Rasmussen Reports, 69 percent of adults feel that cyberbullying should be a punishable crime.

- According to the Cyberbullying Research Center, surveys of law enforcement officers indicate that 85 percent believe cyberbullying reports warrant police attention.

Can Cyberbullying Be Prevented?

Media attention to cyberbullying cases has brought efforts to develop programs aimed at preventing cyberbullying and providing support for victims. These programs are of varying effectiveness, and critics have suggested that many are not worth the effort it takes to create and implement them. Others believe they are generally quite helpful.

One of the best-known support programs is the It Gets Better campaign, created in 2010 by syndicated columnist Dan Savage and his partner, Terry Miller. Their goal is to let gay and lesbian teens know that even if they are being bullied or cyberbullied their lives will eventually get better. The program started with a You-Tube video that was created to help spread this message. The video aims to prevent teen suicides, raise public awareness on the issue of gay and lesbian bullying, and perhaps persuade potential cyber-bullies that engaging in such behavior is wrong. Dozens of celebrities, sports figures, politicians, and other prominent people have made their own It Gets Better videos as well. As of August 2013 there were more than fifty thousand such videos that had been viewed more than 50 million times.

A Combined Effort

The White House launched its own prevention effort in March 2011 by bringing together cyberbullying experts, students, teachers, and parents to discuss prevention-related issues. At the outset of the Bullying Prevention Summit, US president Barack Obama said, "If there's one goal of this conference, it's to dispel the myth that bullying is just a harmless rite of passage or an inevitable part of growing up. It's not."[74]

In conjunction with this event, Facebook announced that it intended to combat cyberbullying by providing a way to report offensive or abusive material that appears on its site. This is the system that still exists today. After the user clicks a button to report the material, the user sees a series of screens. These offer different choices for providing more details about the problem and how the user wants to proceed. For example, the user can indicate whether the material is bullying or harassing the user, whether the user wants to send a message to the person who posted the material, whether the user wants to block this person (making the person invisible to the user while on Facebook), and whether the user wants to get help from a trusted friend in regard to this incident. In regard to the latter, if the user says help is needed, then a screen prompts the user to enter the e-mail address of a friend and compose a message to that friend such as, "Carolyn keeps calling me names online and at school. I want her to stop, but I'm not sure what to do. Can you help?"[75] A copy of the offending material can be forwarded to the friend along with this message.

About this contact-a-friend feature, Facebook states:

> We encourage people on Facebook to use the report buttons located across our site to let us know if they find content that violates our terms of use so we can take it down. But taking down harassing online comments won't necessarily help people solve the underlying problem in the offline world. Social reporting is a way for people to quickly and easily ask for help from someone they trust. Safety and child psychology experts tell us that online issues are frequently a reflection of what is happening offline. By encouraging people to seek help from friends, we hope that many of these situations can be resolved face-to-face.[76]

"If there's one goal of this conference, it's to dispel the myth that bullying is just a harmless rite of passage or an inevitable part of growing up. It's not."[74]

— US president Barack Obama at the March 2011 Bullying Prevention Summit.

Turning to Technology

However, many people believe that Facebook is doing a poor job of acting on reports of problematic content. Therefore, computer experts have been working to develop other ways to prevent offensive material from getting on such sites in the first place. For example, Henry Lieberman, a computer scientist at the Massachusetts Institute of Technology Media Lab whose specialty is artificial intelligence, created word recognition software called BullySpace with the help of his graduate students. This knowledge base has been programmed to recognize certain words, phrases, and combi-

Lady Gaga, performing in Canada in 2011, is one of dozens of celebrities who have made It Gets Better videos aimed at preventing suicide among gay and lesbian teens who have been bullied online or in person.

nations of words and phrases that suggest that they are being used to hurt people.

The software also recognizes gender differences and stereotypes in regard to bullying. Emily Bazelon of the *Atlantic*, who met with Lieberman to discuss BullySpace, provides an example of how this works: "To code for anti-gay taunts, Lieberman included in his knowledge base the fact that 'Put on a wig and lipstick to be who you really are' is more likely to be an insult if directed at a boy. BullySpace understands that lipstick is more often used by girls; it also recognizes more than two hundred other assertions based on stereotypes about gender and sexuality. Lieberman isn't endorsing the stereotypes, of course; he's harnessing them to make BullySpace smarter."[77]

Lieberman is developing other tools to prevent cyberbullying. One of these would use word recognition to trigger a delay in posting. Bazelon explains: "Think about the kid who posted 'Because he's a fag! ROTFL [rolling on the floor laughing]!!!' What if, when he pushed the button to submit, a box popped up saying 'Waiting 60 seconds to post,' next to another box that read 'I don't want to post' and offered a big X to click on? Or what if the message read 'That sounds harsh! Are you sure you want to send that?' Or what if it simply reminded the poster that his comment was about to go to thousands of people?"[78]

Lieberman is mindful that teens might perceive such messages, which have not yet been tested, as a joke. Therefore, he plans to determine their effectiveness by soliciting feedback from teens. He is also concerned that BullySpace could be used to hamper free speech, and he does not want to see this happen. He says, "With spam, okay, you write the program to just automatically delete it. But with bullying, we're talking about free speech. We don't want to censor kids, or ban them from a site." Instead, he envisions the administrators of a site using BullySpace to monitor behavior and step in to intervene when bullying occurs. As an example of how this might work, he explains: "The week before prom, every year, you can see a spike in bullying against LGBT [lesbian, gay, bisexual, and transgendered] kids.

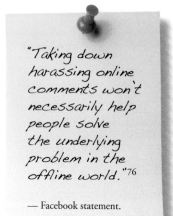

"Taking down harassing online comments won't necessarily help people solve the underlying problem in the offline world."[76]

— Facebook statement.

A Hate Crime

The It Gets Better Project has been creating antibullying videos since 2010. One of the inspirations for this project was the September 2010 suicide of eighteen-year-old Tyler Clementi. Clementi was a student at Rutgers University in New Jersey when his roommate, Dharun Ravi, and a fellow student, Molly Wei, used a webcam to spy on him while he was being affectionate with a man. The two had been alerted to Clementi's meeting with his friend when Clementi asked Ravi to absent himself from the room. After this happened twice, Ravi planned a viewing party for the next time Clementi and his friend were scheduled to meet, telling friends how to access the webcam's images. By this time, Clementi had seen one of Ravi's tweets in which he told others about the webcam. Consequently, he unplugged the webcam and reported Ravi's actions to a school representative, later posting online that the representative had seemed to take his complaint seriously. Nonetheless, fifteen hours after writing this post Clementi jumped off the George Washington Bridge. In March 2012 Ravi was convicted of a hate crime for intimidating Clementi for being gay. (Wei was spared prosecution by agreeing to testify against Ravi.)

With our tool, you can analyze how that spreads—you can make an epidemiological map. And then the social-network site can . . . trace the outbreak back to its source."[79] In this way the site can identify the bullies and warn them that unless they change their behavior they will experience a temporary disruption in service.

Public Embarrassment

A different approach to prevention comes from the world of hackers—computer experts best known for accessing supposedly secure websites to acquire sensitive information. However, members of one of the most prominent hacker groups, Anonymous, are sympathetic to the plight of victims and have helped identify some of their attackers. As part of these efforts, Anonymous launched #OpAntiBully, which seeks to identify and expose cyberbullies in ways that are so punitive and well publicized that others will be dissuaded from engaging in cyberbullying.

An example of this is a case of a twelve-year-old girl being bullied via Twitter by a group of teenage boys. They targeted her after she followed one of the boys, whom she did not know, on Twitter and then unfollowed him after he posted something she did not like. The boys then threatened to rape her, told her to kill herself, and tweeted many other horrible remarks. After noticing the bullying on Twitter, a member of Anonymous using the pseudonym Ash figured out that they attended high school in Abilene, Texas, learned their names, and released this information in an online public forum along with a scathing message to them that said in part, "I am sick of seeing people who think they can get away with breaking someone's confidence and planting seeds of self-hate into someone's head. . . . If you are vile enough to do so and stupid enough to do so on a public forum, such as a social website, then you should know this. . . . We will find you and we will highlight your despicable behavior for all to see."[80]

Almost immediately the boys began receiving messages from people who had read Ash's words; hundreds ultimately condemned their actions. The boys were shocked and upset over this public reaction. It also made them realize that what they had originally viewed as a joke was considered horribly wrong by others.

Education Programs

Others believe that education programs provided by schools can have the most effect because these can start when potential bullies are young. The National Education Association (NEA) has stated that the most effective antibullying programs are those that educate children as they begin learning how to get along with others.

"If you are vile enough to [cyberbully] and stupid enough to do so on a public forum, such as a social website, then you should know this. . . . We will find you and we will highlight your despicable behavior for all to see."[80]

— A member of the hacker group Anonymous.

Meline Kevorkian, author of *101 Facts About Bullying: What Everyone Should Know*, agrees, saying that such programs should start in preschool and kindergarten. At this point, she says, teachers can emphasize the message of "If you don't have something nice to say, don't say anything at all."[81]

Many experts say that it is important to work with schools to tailor a program to the needs at that school. This means finding out which kids are the most likely to be bullied and incorporating that information into the education of school staff, students, and parents on how and when to intervene. Such programs also show all parties how to work together to change beliefs, behaviors, and social norms at the school in order to foster support and trust. In addition, schools might offer classes in responsible and safe computer use.

Some education programs also address an often forgotten factor in bullying: the innocent bystander. This is someone who is present during the bullying but is neither the bully nor the bul-

Members of the hacker group Anonymous (shown here wearing their trademark masks) have launched a campaign to identify and publicly expose cyberbullies. The aim is to dissuade would-be cyberbullies from engaging in such behavior.

lied. Experts believe that such individuals should be encouraged to step forward to defend those who are being bullied. To help innocent bystanders, as well as victims, respond appropriately to bullies, antibullying programs might provide young people with scripted responses; by talking to teens and studying the way they interact with one another, social scientists have determined what kind of language is the most helpful. Many say that the best way for a victim to begin a discussion with a bully is by focusing on how the bullying made the victim feel.

Cutting Off Access

In 2012 Justin W. Patchin and Sameer Hinduja reported that it is hard to determine whether school-based prevention programs work and, if they do, which kinds work best. They say, "More research is needed to fully understand 'what works.' No thorough evaluations of any comprehensive cyberbullying initiative have occurred as yet, and while some programs that focus on bullying more broadly have been reviewed, evidence has been mixed."[82]

However, teens have told researchers what they think works, and it is generally not school-based prevention programs. Instead, teens think it is the threat of taking away a cyberbully's access to electronic communication that would have the most influence on changing his or her behavior. Cyberbullying experts Ellen M. Kraft and Jinchang Wang of the Richard Stockton College of New Jersey report, "Teens perceived the theme of taking away the offender's access to technology as an effective prevention measure, regardless of their roles in cyber bullying. This finding makes sense as all teenagers . . . use these items everyday and would miss them if they were taken away."[83]

Moreover, Kraft and Wang add that "having these personal possessions taken away by their parents, even for a short period of time, would cause them to lose their social status within their peer group. So even though the argument could be made that if a teen's cell phone or computer were taken away they could use a friend's

"When criminals are convicted, often the items used in the commission of the crime are seized and forfeited. . . . Why [should] students, when they plead 'no contest' or 'guilty' to the commission of a cyberbullying offense, be any different?"[85]

— Attorney Parry Aftab.

technology or go to a public library, losing the technological convenience and the stigma would indeed serve as a punishment."[84]

Because teens value their electronic devices so much, Parry Aftab believes that confiscating these devices should be routine in criminal cases where someone has been convicted of cyberbullying. She argues:

> When criminals are convicted, often the items used in the commission of the crime are seized and forfeited. Jet boats and aircraft, million dollar mansions, motorcycles and sports cars are auctioned off by law enforcement authorities after being seized. Why [should] students, when they plead 'no contest' or 'guilty' to the commission of a cyberbullying offense, be any different? Why should their XBox accounts or their Facebook profiles remain their own? Cell phones, gaming devices and laptops are the cyberbullying crime equivalent of the mansions, boats and planes. Why not forfeit them?[85]

Knowing that this would always be a punishment for cyberbullying, she and others suggest, could act as a deterrent to other teens who might be prone to cyberbullying.

Zero Tolerance

Another form of punishment that is already being used to fight cyberbullying is school suspensions. For example, in 2010 a middle school in Seattle, Washington, suspended twenty-eight students in connection with the cyberbullying of a classmate via a Facebook page. The suspensions ranged from two to eight days, depending on the level of involvement.

Many people applauded this punishment as being a good way to show zero tolerance for bullying. This action, they felt, would deter other students from engaging in the same behavior. In fact, teens punished in this way for other cyberbullying incidents have said the suspension did them good, because it made them realize that they really had done something wrong. One San Francisco, California, high school student who received a three-day suspension for creating a fake Facebook page to ridicule another student

Students Against Being Bullied

Sometimes teens will band together to fight cyberbullying among their peers. This is the case with members of the group Students Against Being Bullied (S.A.B.B.), which was founded by sixteen-year-old Ashley Craig of Jefferson Township, New Jersey. Craig had been bullied during seventh grade, and in eighth grade she had gotten help from a school guidance counselor for a suicidal friend. These two events convinced her to dedicate herself to helping others who were having problems at school. The group addresses both face-to-face bullying and cyberbullying, and it encourages victims to text a school counselor when they are being bullied or witness bullying. S.A.B.B. has also worked to set up antibullying support groups where teens can discuss their problems with one another and "safe rooms" in schools where students can go if they do not feel safe in the school's hallways. In addition, S.A.B.B. has a website, www.studentsagainstbeing bullied.org, that provides information on its antibullying programs. These were created for high school students, but S.A.B.B. is currently developing versions for middle schools and elementary schools as well.

said of his punishment, "Basically it's like a slap on wrist for that first time. I don't think what I did was the worst thing in the world. I learned from it, and I haven't done something like that since."[86]

But in regard to the Seattle suspensions, some people criticized the principle of the middle school for suspending so many students so quickly, especially since the bullying took place only off-campus and only involved comments on one Facebook page. Blogger Jim Rest says, "Here's a perfect example of how we have gone overboard in this country when it comes to protecting our kids from the real world. . . . We have all been bullied one time or another, and as far as I remember, as long as it wasn't on school grounds, the school had no authority to be involved. For the school to decide arbitrarily that it has some sort of jurisdiction here makes no sense to me."[87]

Others note that when schools have a zero tolerance policy in regard to bullying, administrators eager to punish all offenders can sometimes treat students who have only a minor role in the bullying more harshly than they deserve. Moreover, the severity of the punishment delivered can also depend on how much publicity the cyberbullying incident has received. This is true not only in schools but in the court system as well. As Aftab explains, "Prosecutors either decide that there is no case, or none worth prosecuting, or throw the book at the cyberbullies. And, in some cases, the only difference between the two is whether or not the community has faced negative cyberbullying publicity or experienced a cyberbullycide [a suicide resulting from cyberbullying]."[88]

A Community Approach

Adding to the problem of determining punishments is the fact that it can be difficult to determine exactly who the true bullies are in an incident where nasty remarks are flying back and forth. As Wayne MacKay, a law professor in Nova Scotia and the chair of a government task force on cyberbullying, reports, "Sometimes the bystanders become the bullies, sometimes the victims become the bullies, the line between all of it is quite complicated." Consequently, MacKay favors an approach to bullying that relies primarily on teaching young people how to use computers responsibly so that they can become good citizens in the online world, especially since "any study looking at cyberbullying suggests you can't simply demonize the bullies and say they should be sent off to some island somewhere and they're a separate species."[89]

For this reason, many experts suggest that the best way to prevent cyberbullying is by reminding people that they are part of a community wherein individuals need to respect and support one another. One way to do

"We have all been bullied one time or another, and as far as I remember, as long as it wasn't on school grounds, the school had no authority to be involved."[87]

— Blogger Jim Rest.

this is by working to combat mean-spiritedness, intolerance, and prejudices in the media and society at large, to make it clear that it is always wrong—both offline and online—for one person to treat another unkindly, even under the pretenses that "it's just a joke." Another way is to require anyone who hurts others online to repair that hurt by working to directly help the victim. This approach, which is gaining ground in legal circles but is rarely put into practice, is called restorative justice.

Aftab explains that restorative justice, which she says could also be called "Clean Up The Mess You Made," would require cyberbullies to work to undo the damage they have caused by trying to eliminate or counter any remarks they made or images they shared in their efforts to hurt the victim. As an example, she says: "The same 'mean girls' who defamed their target with false rumors about her promiscuity can help turn things around with texts and IMs sent to everyone they sent the original statements to, telling them that what they did was wrong and asking others to delete anything they had and to forward this to others they may have shared the derogatory statements with." However, she adds that cyberbullies should not be trusted to do this without someone overseeing their work. She explains, "Supervision is crucial to make sure that the apology is genuine and this is not used to further the attacks."[90]

Because of this risk, many judges are more comfortable sentencing cyberbullies to perform community service unrelated to their specific attacks. However, some people have argued that this service should always involve promoting an antibullying message, much the way teenage drunk drivers who have killed someone might be ordered to participate in anti–drunk driving assemblies at schools. Such assemblies allow offending teens to express remorse and speak of how their actions impacted the lives not just of themselves but of their victims.

But those who favor antibullying assemblies acknowledge that these are only one of many tools that must be used to combat cyberbullying. They also know that even the most powerful words of remorse might not be enough to stop some young people from

"Sometimes the bystanders become the bullies, sometimes the victims become the bullies, the line between all of it is quite complicated."[89]

— Wayne MacKay, the chair of a Nova Scotia task force on cyberbullying.

harassing others online. Still, many feel that everything that can be tried should be tried in order to prevent cyberbullying. Otherwise it might become an acceptable practice among teens who would then carry this behavior into adulthood.

Facts

- Connecticut's *Hartford County Examiner* reported in 2010 that only 15 percent of parents were aware of their children's social networking habits.

- The global research company Ipsos reports that based on online surveys of people in twenty-four countries, 66 percent of adults worldwide are aware that cyberbullying is a significant problem; in the United States 82 percent consider it a problem.

- In a 2010 online survey by Care.com, an organization that assists families with caregiving issues, 20 percent of parents graded their children's schools a D or F when it came to their antibullying education efforts.

- According to a poll conducted online by the global research company Ipsos as reported in January 2012, only 23 percent of parents around the world who use the Internet believe that cyberbullying is being adequately handled through existing antibullying efforts.

- In a 2010 study conducted by Iowa State University, 80 percent of young people said that their peers should do more to stop cyberbullying; only 48 percent said the government needed to do more.

Source Notes

Introduction: New Ways to Bully

1. Quoted in Elizabeth Landau, "When Bullying Goes High-Tech," CNN, April 15, 2013. www.cnn.com.
2. Quoted in Jennifer L. Thornhill and Bobbie Mixon, "Recognizing a Cyberbully," National Science Foundation, November 15, 2011. www.nsf.gov.
3. Quoted in Phil McKenna, "The Rise of Cyber-Bullying," *Reader's Digest*, September 8, 2010. www.readersdigest.com.au.
4. Lisa Belkin, "When Mommies Are Bullies," *Motherlode* (blog), *New York Times*, January 27, 2010. http://parenting.blogs.nytimes.com.
5. Quoted in Patrick Sawer, "Cyberbullying Victims Speak Out: 'They Were Anonymous So They Thought They Could Get Away with It,'" *Telegraph* (London), November 13, 2011. www.telegraph.co.uk.
6. Quoted in Thornhill and Mixon, "Recognizing a Cyberbully."
7. Quoted in Thornhill and Mixon, "Recognizing a Cyberbully."
8. Quoted in Sawer, "Cyberbullying Victims Speak Out."
9. Quoted in Sawer, "Cyberbullying Victims Speak Out."
10. Quoted in Landau, "When Bullying Goes High-Tech."
11. Quoted in Landau, "When Bullying Goes High-Tech."

Chapter One: What Are the Origins of Cyberbullying?

12. Quoted in Chris Taylor, "'Star Wars Kid' Blasts Bullies, Jedi Knights Defend Him," Mashable, May 10, 2013. http://mashable.com.
13. Quoted in Taylor, "'Star Wars Kid' Blasts Bullies."
14. Quoted in McKenna, "The Rise of Cyber-Bullying."
15. Quoted in Julia Harris, "Sexting, Cyber Bullies, and Textual Harassment," *Cartersville Patch*, May 17, 2011. http://cartersville.patch.com.
16. Quoted in Jennifer Steinhauer, "Woman Who Posed as Boy Testifies in Case That Ended in Suicide of 13-Year-Old," *New York Times*, November 20, 2008. www.nytimes.com.
17. Quoted in Steinhauer, "Woman Who Posed as Boy Testifies in Case That Ended in Suicide of 13-Year-Old."
18. Quoted in Associated Press, "Missouri Passes Law Criminalizing Cyber Harassment," Fox News, May 16, 2008. www.foxnews.com.

19. Quoted in Fox News "Missouri Passes Law Criminalizing Cyber Harassment."

20. Ashley Surdin, "In Several States, a Push to Stem Cyber-Bullying," *Washington Post*, January 1, 2009. http://articles.washingtonpost .com.

21. Quoted in Surdin, "In Several States, a Push to Stem Cyber-Bullying."

22. Quoted in Sharon Jayson, "Studies Show Cyberbullying Concerns Have Been Overstated," *USA Today*, August 4, 2012. http://usatoday 30.usatoday.com.

23. Quoted in Jayson, "Studies Show Cyberbullying Concerns Have Been Overstated."

24. Quoted in Stuart Wolpert, "Bullying of Teenagers Online Is Common, UCLA Psychologists Report," UCLA Newsroom, October 2, 2008. http://newsroom.ucla.edu.

25. Quoted in Wolpert, "Bullying of Teenagers Online Is Common, UCLA Psychologists Report."

Chapter Two: Why and How Do People Bully Others Online?

26. Kris Varjas, Jasmaine Talley, Joel Meyers, Leandra Parris, and Haley Cutts, "High School Students' Perceptions of Motivations for Cyberbullying: An Exploratory Study," Georgia State University Center for School Safety, School Climate, and Classroom Management, *Western Journal of Emergency Medicine*, vol. 11, no. 3, August 2010, p. 270.

27. Quoted in Varjas et al., "High School Students' Perceptions of Motivations for Cyberbullying," p. 271.

28. Quoted in Varjas et al., "High School Students' Perceptions of Motivations for Cyberbullying," p. 271.

29. Quoted in Varjas et al., "High School Students' Perceptions of Motivations for Cyberbullying," p. 272.

30. Varjas, Talley et al., "High School Students' Perceptions of Motivations for Cyberbullying," p. 270.

31. Quoted in Stuart Wolpert, "'Cool' Kids in Middle School Bully More, UCLA Psychologists Report," UCLA Newsroom, January 24, 2013. http://newsroom.ucla.edu.

32. Quoted in Dhwani Shah, "JuicyCampus Gushes Gossip," *Daily Princetonian*, February 22, 2008. www.dailyprincetonian.com.

33. Quoted in Shah, "JuicyCampus Gushes Gossip."

34. Quoted in Shah, "JuicyCampus Gushes Gossip."

35. Quoted in Ben Chapman and Christina Boyle, "Staten Island Teen Amanda Cummings Kills Self by Jumping in Front of a Bus After Being Bullied," *New York Daily News*, January 3, 2012. www.nydaily news.com.

36. Quoted in Justin Sarachik, "Amanda Cummings Victim of Cyber Bullying and Mockery Even After Death," *Christian Post*, January 6, 2012. www.christianpost.com.

37. Quoted in Sarachik, "Amanda Cummings Victim of Cyber Bullying and Mockery Even After Death."

38. Glen Canning, "Rehtaeh Parsons Was My Daughter," *Glen Canning's Blog*, April 10, 2013. http://glencanning.com.

39. Quoted in Emily Bazelon, "Non-Consensual Sexting Leads to Child Pornography Charges for Two Men in Rehtaeh Parsons Case," *Slate*, August 8, 2013. www.slate.com.

Chapter Three: How Does Cyberbullying Affect Victims?

40. Quoted in Dawn Gagnon, "Former Orono High Student Charged in Cyberbullying Case; Target and Family Speak Out," *Bangor (ME) Daily News*, November 15, 2012. https://bangordailynews.com.

41. Quoted in Gagnon, "Former Orono High Student Charged in Cyberbullying Case."

42. Quoted in Gagnon, "Former Orono High Student Charged in Cyberbullying Case."

43. Quoted in Dawn Gagnon, "Teen Cyberbully Pleads Guilty to Terrorizing Former Orono Schoolmate," *Bangor (ME) Daily News*, March 26, 2013. http://bangordailynews.com.

44. Quoted in Gagnon, "Teen Cyberbully Pleads Guilty to Terrorizing Former Orono Schoolmate."

45. Quoted in Gagnon, "Teen Cyberbully Pleads Guilty to Terrorizing Former Orono Schoolmate."

46. Kelsey Kangos, "I Was Cyberbullied," *Thought Catalog*, May 28, 2013. http://thoughtcatalog.com.

47. Kangos, "I Was Cyberbullied."

48. Kangos, "I Was Cyberbullied."

49. Quoted in Kay Stephens, "Finding Balance in the Media Hype About the Connection Between Cyberbullying and Suicide," *Boothbay (ME) Register*, June 19, 2013. www.boothbayregister.com.

50. Paul Butler, "Not Every Tragedy Should Lead to Prison," Room for Debate, *New York Times*, September 30, 2010. www.nytimes.com.

51. Quoted in Stephens, "Finding Balance in the Media Hype About the Connection Between Cyberbullying and Suicide."

52. Quoted in Sameer Hinduja and Justin W. Patchin, "Cyberbullying Research Summary: Emotional and Psychological Consequences," Cyberbullying Research Center, 2009. www.cyberbullying.us.

53. Quoted in Hinduja and Patchin, "Cyberbullying Research Summary."

54. Quoted in McKenna, "The Rise of Cyber-Bullying."

55. Quoted in McKenna, "The Rise of Cyber-Bullying."
56. Hinduja and Patchin, "Cyberbullying Research Summary."
57. Susan Arnout Smith, "The Fake Facebook Profile I Could Not Get Removed," *Salon*, February 1, 2011. www.salon.com.
58. Smith, "The Fake Facebook Profile I Could Not Get Removed."
59. Smith, "The Fake Facebook Profile I Could Not Get Removed."

Chapter Four: How Effective Are Cyberbullying Laws?

60. Quoted in Greg Bluestein and Dorie Turner, "School Cyberbullying Victims Fight Back in Lawsuits," *Huffington Post*, April 26, 2012. www.huffingtonpost.com.
61. Quoted in Yesenia Robles, "15-Year-Old Charged in Arvada Cyberbullying Case," *Denver Post*, January 26, 2013. www.denverpost.com.
62. Quoted in Andrew Carswell, "Parents Take Extreme Action on Faceless Bullying," *Daily Telegraph* (London), May 20, 2013. http://dailytelegraph.com.au.
63. Quoted in Barbie Latza Nadeau, "Italy's Tragic Teen Cyberbullying Suicide," *Daily Beast*, May 31, 2013. www.thedailybeast.com.
64. Quoted in Nadeau, "Italy's Tragic Teen Cyberbullying Suicide."
65. Quoted in Emma Barnett and Iain Hollingshead, "The Dark Side of Facebook," *Telegraph* (London), March 2, 2012. www.telegraph.co.uk.
66. Barnett and Hollingshead, "The Dark Side of Facebook."
67. Anna North, "Is Legislation the Way to Stop Cyberbullying?," *Jezebel*, October 1, 2009. http://jezebel.com.
68. Sameer Hinduja and Justin W. Patchin, "Cyberbullying Fact Sheet: A Brief Review of Relevant Legal and Policy Issues," Cyberbullying Research Center, 2009. www.cyberbullying.us.
69. Quoted in Elbert Chu, "Should Cyberbullying Be a Crime?," WNYC, April 27, 2012. www.wnyc.org.
70. Quoted in Chu, "Should Cyberbullying Be a Crime?"
71. Quoted in Chu, "Should Cyberbullying Be a Crime?"
72. Quoted in Kerri Winick, "Cyber Bullies: Evidence WOMEN Are 'Meaner' than GIRLS," GALTime.com, August 10, 2010. http://shine.yahoo.com.
73. North, "Is Legislation the Way to Stop Cyberbullying?"

Chapter Five: Can Cyberbullying Be Prevented?

74. Barack Obama, "President Obama and the First Lady at the White House Conference on Cyberbullying Prevention," White House, March 10, 2011. www.whitehouse.gov.
75. Facebook, "Details on Social Reporting," March 10, 2011. www.facebook.com.

76. Facebook, "Details on Social Reporting."
77. Emily Bazelon, "How to Stop the Bullies," *Atlantic,* February 20, 2013. www.theatlantic.com.
78. Bazelon, "How to Stop the Bullies."
79. Quoted in Bazelon, "How to Stop the Bullies."
80. Quoted in Bazelon, "How to Stop the Bullies."
81. Quoted in Mary Ellen Flannery, "Bullying: Does It Get Better?," National Education Association, December 2010. www.nea.org.
82. Justin W. Patchin and Sameer Hinduja, "School-Based Efforts to Prevent Cyberbullying," *Prevention Researcher*, vol. 19, no. 3, September 2012, p. 9.
83. Ellen M. Kraft and Jinchang Wang, "Effectiveness of Cyber Bullying Prevention Strategies: A Study on Students' Perspectives," *International Journal of Cyber Criminology*, vol. 3, no. 2, July/December 2009, p. 530.
84. Kraft and Wang, "Effectiveness of Cyber Bullying Prevention Strategies," p. 530.
85. Parry Aftab, "Clean Up Your Mess! Restorative Justice and the Alternative Judicial Remedies for Cyberbullying Cases," *Parry Aftab's Blog*, August 15, 2013. http://parryaftab.blogspot.com.
86. Quoted in Cooper Logan, "Cyberbullying: How Schools Cope with the Online Threat," *Lowell*, April 26, 2012. www.thelowell.org.
87. Jim Rest, "Local News: Cyberbullying Leads to a Suspension of 28 Middle-Schoolers at McClure: *Seattle Times Newspaper*," *blog.jimr.me*, January 16, 2010. http://blog.jimr.me.
88. Aftab, "Clean Up Your Mess!"
89. Quoted in CBC News, "N.S. Cyberbullying Legislation Allows Victims to Sue," August 7, 2013. http://ca.news.yahoo.com.
90. Aftab, "Clean Up Your Mess!"

Related Organizations and Websites

Center for Democracy and Technology (CDT)
1634 I St. NW, #1100
Washington, DC 20006
phone: (202) 637-9800
website: www.cdt.org

A nonprofit public policy organization, the CDT promotes freedom of expression, freedom of the Internet, and other civil liberties. Its website offers information on a variety of Internet-related issues, including cyberbullying.

Center for Safe and Responsible Internet Use
474 W. Twenty-Ninth Ave.
Eugene, OR 97405
phone: (541) 556-1145
e-mail: contact@csriu.org
website: www.cyberbully.org

Established by Internet safety expert Nancy Willard, the Center for Safe and Responsible Internet Use offers reports and guides that address issues arising from the use of the Internet in schools, including cyberbullying.

Community Matters
652 Petaluma Ave., Suite J-1
PO Box 14816
Santa Rosa, CA 95402
phone: (707) 823-6159
e-mail: team@community-matters.org
website: www.community-matters.org

This group works with schools and communities to prevent violence. To this end, its website provides information on how to stop school bullying.

Cyberbullying Research Center

e-mail: info@cyberbullying.us
website: www.cyberbullying.us

The Cyberbullying Research Center provides a wealth of information on cyberbullying. Its website has many resources for educators, parents, and teens and includes victims' stories.

DoSomething.org

website: www.dosomething.org

A nonprofit organization, DoSomething.org spearheads national campaigns that provide ways for thirteen- to twenty-five-year-olds to make a different in the world. Among its causes are bullying and cyberbullying, and its website provides information on both.

End to Cyber Bullying (ETCB)

phone: (772) 202-3822
e-mail: info@endcyberbullying.org
website: www.endcyberbullying.org

A nonprofit organization, the ETC is dedicated to raising awareness on issues related to cyberbullying and to creating a global social networking arena that is free of cyberbullying. Its website provides information on cyberbullying and resources to help victims, including online counseling.

Enough Is Enough

746 Walker Rd., Suite 116
Great Falls, VA 22066
phone: (703) 476-7890
websites: www.enough.org; http://internetsafety101.org

Enough Is Enough works toward making the Internet safer for children and families. To this end it produced the Internet Safety 101 teaching series for schools, and its website provides information on a variety of Internet dangers, including cyberbullying.

Family Online Safety Institute (FOSI)

624 Ninth St. NW, Suite 222
Washington, DC 20001
phone: (202) 572-6252
e-mail: fosi@fosi.org
website: http://fosi.org

An international nonprofit organization, FOSI partners with major communications and entertainment companies to develop a safer Internet while still respecting free speech. It also works with Internet safety advocates and others to develop new technology, shape public policy, and promote education related to online safety. Its website provides information on such issues as cyberbullying and sexting.

It Gets Better

The It Gets Better Project
110 S. Fairfax Ave., Suite A11-71
Los Angeles, CA 90036
website: www.itgetsbetter.org

This organization is behind the It Gets Better Project, which creates videos reassuring lesbian, gay, bisexual, and transgender youth around the world that their lives will eventually get better even if they are being bullied and encouraging them to work toward making changes that will help improve their lives right now.

National Crime Prevention Council

2001 Jefferson Davis Hwy., Suite 901
Arlington, VA 22202-4801
phone: (202) 466-6272
website: www.ncpc.org

The National Crime Prevention Council provides communities with resources to help them prevent crime. Its website includes information on cyberbullying, including tips on how to prevent it and respond to it.

STOMP Out Bullying™

220 E. Fifty-Seventh St., 9th Floor, Suite G
New York, NY 10022-2820
phone: (877) 602-8559
website: www.stompoutbullying.org

STOMP Out Bullying™ is a national antibullying and cyberbullying organization for children and teens in the United States. It works toward reducing and preventing cyberbullying, sexting, and other forms of digital abuse, and its website provides information intended to educate young people in how to deal with these problems.

StopBullying

website: www.stopbullying.gov

On its website, StopBullying offers bullying- and cyberbullying-related information provided by various government agencies. This includes advice on how to prevent cyberbullying, how to respond to cyberbullying, and who is most at risk of being cyberbullied.

Teens of America

phone: (877) 333-8200
website: www.teensofamerica.net

A nonprofit organization, Teens of America is dedicated to educating America's young people on issues related to substance abuse and crime. In regard to the latter, its website includes teens' true stories of dealing with such problems as bullying, cyberbullying, and sexting.

Web Wise Kids

website: www.webwisekids.org

Founded in 2000 and currently part of the US federal government's Project Safe Childhood initiative, Web Wise Kids is a national nonprofit organization dedicated to empowering young people to make wise choices online. Its programs help children deal with issues such as sexting, cyberbullying, Internet fraud, and online sexual predation.

Wired Safety

website: www.wiredsafety.org

Founded in 1995, the nonprofit group Wired Safety helps victims of cybercrime and online harassment, assists law enforcement worldwide in preventing and investigating cybercrimes, and disseminates information designed to educate people on privacy, security, and other aspects of online safety.

Additional Reading

Lorna Blumen, *Bullying Epidemic: Not Just Child's Play.* Toronto, ON: Camberley, 2010.

Naomi Drew, *No Kidding About Bullying.* Minneapolis, MN: Free Spirit, 2010.

Lauri S. Friedman, ed., *Cyberbullying.* Farmington Hills, MI: Greenhaven, 2011.

Matt Ivester, *lol . . . OMG!: What Every Student Needs to Know About Online Reputation Management, Digital Citizenship, and Cyberbullying.* Reno, NV: Serra Knight, 2011.

Thomas A. Jacobs, *Teen Cyberbullying Investigated: Where Do Your Rights End and Consequences Begin?* Minneapolis, MN: Free Spirit, 2010.

Robin M. Kowalski, Susan P. Limber, and Patricia W. Agatston, *Cyberbullying: Bullying in the Digital Age.* Oxford, UK: Wiley-Blackwell, 2012.

Qing Li, Donna Cross, and Peter K. Smith, eds., *Cyberbullying in the Global Playground: Research from International Perspectives.* Oxford, UK: Wiley-Blackwell, 2012.

Raychelle Cassada Lohmann and Julia V. Taylor, *The Bullying Workbook for Teens: Activities to Help You Deal with Social Aggression and Cyberbullying.* Oakland, CA: Instant Help, 2013.

Robyn MacEachern and Geraldine Charette, *Cyberbullying: Deal with It and Ctrl Alt Delete It.* Toronto, ON: Lorimer, 2011.

Samuel C. McQuade, Sarah Gentry, and Nathan Fisk, *Cyberbullying and Cyberstalking*. New York: Chelsea House, 2011.

Peggy J. Parks, *Cyberbullying*. San Diego, CA: ReferencePoint, 2013.

Peter Ryan, *Online Bullying*. New York: Rosen, 2010.

Kay Stephens, *Cyberslammed: Understand, Prevent, Combat and Transform the Most Common Cyberbullying Tactics*. Rockland, ME: sMashup, 2012.

Index

Note: Boldface page numbers indicate illustrations.

Picture Credits

About the Author

Patricia D. Netzley is the author of more than fifty books for children, teens, and adults. She also teaches writing and knitting and is a member of the Society of Children's Book Writers and Illustrators.

Perkins County Schools
PO Box 829
Grant NE 69140-0829